Rooting Out Shame

A Son's Account of Child Sexual Abuse and Recovery

FRANK ROOT III

FOREWORD BY JESSICA E. MIRANDA

PDW
Pedos Don't Win
Benson, Arizona

Published by: Pedos Don't Win
          1030 Barrel Cactus Ridge, #195
          Benson, AZ 85602
          www.rootingoutshame.com

Editor: Ellen Kleiner
Book design and production: Janice St. Marie

FIRST EDITION

Printed in the United States of America

Publisher's Cataloging-in-Publication Data

Names: Root, Frank, III, author.

Title: Rooting out shame : a son's account of child sexual
          abuse and recovery / Frank Root III.

Description: First edition. | Benson, Arizona : Pedos Don't
              Win, [2025] | Includes bibliographical references.

Identifiers: ISBN: 979-8-9908781-0-5 (paperback) | 979-8-
              9908781-1-2 (ebook) | LCCN: 2024912120

Subjects: LCSH: Root, Frank, III. | Adult child sexual abuse
            victims--Biography. | Sexually abused boys--United
            States--Biography. | Incest victims--Biography. |
            Child molesters--Trials, litigation, etc. | Repression
            (Psychology) | Recovered memory. | Self-care,
            Health. | Child sexual abuse--Psychological aspects.
            | Sexual abuse victims' writings.

Classification: LCC: RC569.5.A28 R66 2025 | DDC:
                  616.85/8369--dc23

1 3 5 7 9 10 8 6 4 2

Praise for *Rooting Out Shame...*

"As is often the case for survivors of sexual trauma, Frank Root's memories lay dormant for decades until one day they suddenly surfaced, painfully and radically changing the trajectory of his life and his wife's. In *Rooting Out Shame*, Frank vulnerably and graphically shares some of the horrific traumas he and his siblings endured at the hands of their perversely abusive parents, and their courageous battle for some semblance of justice. From disruptive flashbacks and fragmented trauma memories, Frank has formed a narrative—a vital part of the healing journey—that is both cohesive and engaging, and now he's helping others do the same."
—ERIKA SHERSHUN, MA, LMFT
Author of the *Healing Sexual Trauma Workbook*
and the *Healing Sexual Trauma Guided Journal*
(www.HealingSexualTrauma.com)

"Vivid, shocking, and blatant, this courageous author describes in detail the thoughts, feelings, and horror from being a victim of parental incest as a young child. After years of repression, he begins his journey of recollection, shame, devastation, and finally healing. Through years of therapy, he describes how he, together with his wife, embraced the emotional and psychological journey of healing to find renewed love, justice, and peace. A must-read for the mental health community who work with families of incest and childhood sexual abuse."
—CAROL L. PETRO, MSW, LSW
Marriage and family specialist

"The author's professionalism and compassionate approach to his friends and family are an inspiration. An incest survivor myself, I'm convinced the steadfast courage he exudes in this book can be a beacon of hope for survivors everywhere. His message is clear and unwavering. The grit and determination revealed in these pages exemplifies the true triumph of the human spirit."

—LIEUTENANT JOHN AMBROSE
Avon Fire Department

"*Rooting Out Shame* is a courageous personal account of the amazing human capacity to transform into an instrument of healing, love, and support despite enduring truly horrific violations of body and mind. This story is a powerful reminder that childhood sexual abuse insidiously manifests in various forms that metastasize in darkness and silence. The author's resilient voice blazes a powerfully enlightening and antidotal pathway toward elevating our human consciousness, empathy, and systems of justice."

—CAITLIN EWING, LPCC
Certified Clinical Trauma Professional
and EMDR Trained Therapist

"It had to have taken enormous bravery to bring forth such a personal story. Clearly, Chief Frank Root III did it in the hope that it would help the men and women who read it. *Rooting Out Shame* is a hard story to read, but a very important one."

—TERRY M. COSTIGAN
TMC News

To my wife Karyn, my rock, my reason for living, my everything. Your love and support are why I was able to tell you about my past and continue on this journey.

To my siblings, Bobbi, Ruth, and Bret. May any child who lives in a house of horrors have siblings like you from whom to gain strength.

And to our children, Kaylee, Frankie, Xavier, Evan, and Alex. May you live in a future where people will not feel the need to repress abuse and where the #metoo movement will continue to give women and men the strength to stand tall.

Acknowledgments

I deeply appreciate the many people who have contributed, in ways visible and invisible, to the creation of this book, including the following:

Karyn Root, my wife and best friend, without whose guidance and encouragement this book would not have been written.

Eric Dudziak, my amazing friend and co-worker, who stood by me throughout my struggles and kept me sane during my final years in the fire service.

Craig Johnson, one of my favorite firefighters, whose support has been unwavering.

Ellen Kleiner, my editor at Blessingway Authors' Services, for believing in me and assuring me that this story needed to be told.

Paul St. Marie, personal attorney and friend, who relentlessly found ways to press charges against my father.

Rhonda Debevec, my civil attorney, who won a seemingly unwinnable case.

Contents

Foreword

Rooting Out Shame is a powerful testimony to the resilience of survivors of child sexual abuse and molestation. More importantly, it is a story that demands to be told—a story of not only suffering but also courage, endurance, and ultimately, healing. In sharing his painful experiences, Frank Root III breaks the silence that has kept so many survivors in the shadows. His bravery echoes the principles of the #MeToo movement, reminding us all of the importance of bringing these issues to light and fostering a society that does not turn a blind eye to abuse.

Frank contacted my office countless times during my term as State Representative in Ohio. He informed my staff that he would be willing to help in any way to end the antiquated statute of limitation laws governing child sexual abuse cases. He offered to testify, call committee chairs, and contact other representatives and senators to further this agenda. He hoped his status as a retired fire chief would help shed light on the issue, which it did, while simultaneously demonstrating his extraordinary integrity and commitment to survivor recovery.

I have often shared my personal story of surviving child sexual abuse and rape in speeches and with the media. These moments were not easy, but they were necessary. They were a step toward healing for me and a call to action for those in positions of power to effect change. Frank's book is a continuation of this call—a summons for renewal and a powerful, unyielding demand for justice and recognition for all survivors. This straight-talking chronicle, with graphic details, delivers a vision of hope grounded in fierce determination. We witness the strength it took for Frank to overcome the horrors he endured, along with the gritty mind-set he cultivated to learn from them and become a better person. While it is easy for abuse survivors to spiral out of control, here we learn how possible it is to instead adapt and overcome.

As you read Frank's story, may you be moved to understand the depth of his experiences and the fortitude it took to share them. His journey is a testament to the indomitable human spirit and the unwavering pursuit of justice. Let his words inspire you to pursue the path to self-healing, support survivors, and advocate for the changes needed to protect and empower them.

—JESSICA E. MIRANDA
Hamilton County (Ohio) Auditor
Former Ohio State Representative, District 28
2024 NSVRC Visionary Voice Award Recipient

Introduction

This book chronicles my gradual recollection of raw, horrific events spanning a decade of repeated child sexual abuse, largely incest, instigated by my parents, and my subsequent fight to heal and seek accountability. Only after spending more than forty years piecing together these disturbing fragments of memories, which surfaced in sporadic flashbacks, can I speak out about the abuse that stole my innocence, shattered my self-esteem, and left me with a deep well of shame I didn't deserve. And while breaking the bonds of silence has been painful, the story is worth telling because it is also about acquiring the strength to speak up, shining light on the great harm sexual exploitation causes children, and encouraging fellow victims to free themselves from the chains of the past.

I never imagined that at age fifty-seven I would be in the situation I now find myself. In September 2018, when I was fifty-two, my world as I knew it came crashing down. A longtime firefighter, I was at work while watching the confirmation hearing of Supreme Court nominee Brett Kavanaugh. At the point where professor Christine Blasey Ford was cross-examined by senators for revealing her previously repressed memories of sexual assault by him when they were in high school, I was outraged to see her treated with disbelief and disdain. Moments later, I felt sure Blasey Ford was being victimized again, this time by the nominee's demeaning testimony, and subsequently by his appointment to the highest court in the land. Having followed the #metoo movement, I'd been glad that actors, movie producers, politicians, and others were being taken to task for sexual assault, but I could not bear seeing this witness courageously come forward only to face endeavors to refute her claim by discrediting her and questioning how memories from so long ago could be trusted. I wondered why the skeptical senators assumed that old memories could not be credible, especially those involving trauma that had obviously left deep emotional scars.

In that instant, I had my first extended flashback of sexual abuse as a child, with images so disgusting I could not believe they included me. The remainder of my workday was taken up by many more such flashbacks. By the end of my shift, I knew I had to break the startling news to my wife, Karyn, that for many years during my childhood I had been molested by my father and mother—a confession I feared would lead to marital problems, as well as personal humiliation or even self-hatred.

That night while we were lying in bed, I was about to tell Karyn about my discovery when she fell fast asleep. Emotionally exhausted, I did too. After about an hour, my phone rang regarding a structure fire, and I prepared to leave but then received a cancellation because the incident was minor. No sooner did I go back to bed than my mind began racing with yet more memories of sexual abuse, causing my emotions to vacillate rapidly between anger and shame. At least another hour passed before I finally mustered the courage to nudge Karyn. "What's wrong?" she asked. I told her that what I had to reveal was bad and, after hearing it, she would have every right to leave me. Finally, after a brief pause, I summoned all my courage and said, "When I was a kid, I was forced to have sex with my mother." Karyn was shocked. I then explained that I had been repressing memories of these incidents for years and would share them with her, to the best of my recollection, as they emerged. In response, my beautiful, perfect wife held me and assured me that everything was going to be okay, that we would get through this and reach out for all the help I needed. I knew that although we faced a long battle, the toughest part was over: I had told my wife the abhorrent truth and she had not abandoned me. In fact, she had responded with love and support, eventually encouraging me to reveal my memories of sexual abuse to the public—and so this book was conceived.

In coming forward to write about my past sexual abuse after all these years, I am not saying I'm a hero. On the contrary, I have been a firefighter and paramedic for thirty-seven years, done some brave things, and know there are individuals alive today because of my actions, all of which is customary for people in this line of work. I was paid to do a job I loved, and I did it well, driven largely by the desire to become a better person than my father. For example, while advancing to company officer and then chief officer, I dealt skillfully with each challenge that came my way, proving to colleagues that I was both good to have at an emergency scene and a man of few fears inside a fire. I also managed to become fairly successful, enhancing my life with not only a fulfilling career but also a beautiful wife and five wonderful children.

Nor do I see myself as a victim. At first I was good at repressing my memories of the sexual events; but as momentary thoughts of them arose in my adult life, they insisted on being noticed, causing me pain, confusion, a distorted view of sex, and inevitably shame, with its tenacious ability to cast a long shadow over my sense of self-worth. Rather than surrender to this crippling condition and risk becoming entombed in depression, I would remind myself of what Robin Williams's character repeatedly told Matt Damon's in the film *Good Will Hunting:* "It's not your fault." Then I would strive to reclaim my resilience by uprooting any residual sense of worthlessness, using a variety of methods I had learned—a practice that continues to restore my sense of agency.

The label I can handle is "survivor." This book was written through the lens of a firefighter emerging from a trying ordeal neither as a superstar nor a casualty of the adversity, but as the harbinger of a better life. To other survivors of child sexual abuse, I say: "Whatever you may be ashamed of or repressing, remember that someone else committed the abuse and that to pursue your dreams you must"—echoing my favorite tenet in the fire service—"adapt and overcome." May you find strategies for doing so in the following chapters. For more support and information, please see the resources listed at the back of the book.

The shame associated with sexual violations in childhood—especially by a parent expected to instead provide love and protection—can have a long-lasting impact on the child's physical, emotional, and mental growth and pose significant challenges in adulthood. Issues of vulnerability and powerlessness may run deep. My wish is that this book will give readers hope in their own struggles and those of others to overcome the debilitating effects of child sexual abuse and help nourish their potential for success in life.

CHAPTER 1

OPENING UP TO MY WIFE, Karyn, about my past sexual abuse at age fifty-two set off a cascade of long-buried memories. After each one, I would flash on a dialogue from the movie *Pulp Fiction*, between Butch, played by Bruce Willis, and Marsellus, performed by Ving Rhames.

Butch: Are we okay?
Marsellus: No, man. I'm pretty fucking far
             from okay.

Now, years later, Marsellus's reply still comes to mind when I'm feeling far from okay. I'm getting much better, but it has been a roller-coaster ride—one perhaps even more horrific than his because my experience of abuse occurred in an unexpected place and time.

Growing up in Avon, Ohio, in the early 1970s usually guaranteed one thing: a simple life. My family lived in a boring, mostly rural community a long way from the suburban sprawl that would later triple the size of the town. Our house, on the west and most rural side of town, was a century-old, modest-size bright red farmhouse on three acres that abutted my paternal grandparents' multi-acre farm and greenhouse. My time was spent mostly with my older sister Ruth and younger brother Bret, fishing at the nearby ponds, cruising on a three-wheel ATV, building massive snow forts in the winter, and swimming in the backyard pool during the summer. My half-sister Bobbi, who lived with my grandparents, did not spend much time with us. There were no incidents of school shootings, mass killings, or domestic terrorism that form the mainstay of today's news. Thoughts of the Cold War with Russia and the Vietnam War were easily dismissed. My one memory of President Nixon comes from the Watergate coverage that interrupted regularly scheduled news broadcasts, forcing an NFL game into overtime or cutting into a children's TV program, like *The Wonderful World of Disney.*

My parents stood in stark contrast to one another. My father, very large at 5 feet 11 inches tall and more than 350 pounds, had brown hair trimmed in a crew cut and wore glasses. He was very strong and, for a man his size, unusually fast. He shaved daily and would leave his whiskers in the bathroom sink for Ruth, Bret, or me to clean out. My mother, on the other hand, was a diminutive 5 feet 2 inches tall and fairly skinny. She wore glasses to help correct a lazy eye and had thinning hair, over which she usually wore a wig. A disastrous homemaker, she never cleaned the house or cooked a palatable meal. While my father was a classic authoritarian, she was a vintage submissive, and no questioning of either one was tolerated. The two would likely not have stayed together had he not gotten her pregnant.

My parents, Ruth, Bret, and I had dinner together as a family almost every night. The atmosphere was usually fairly pleasant, aside from my father's snarky comments about my mother's subpar cooking. Our food choices were limited and of poor quality, due to my father's habit of bringing home items that were out of date, discarded by a grocer, or retrieved from a garbage dumpster. Equally unappetizing, we children, conditioned to eat sparingly, were continually torn between wanting to satisfy our appetites and having to leave at least seconds for our exceedingly overweight father. The five of us would, for instance, have to split a round steak, aged at the butcher shop then cooked by my mother to the consistency of shoe leather. I also recall feeling nauseous from the fumes of baked spareribs served in their own grease. Every meal included mashed potatoes, which, while fine with me, would invariably elicit the same depressing comment from my father: "Mashed potatoes again. May wonders never cease." Immediately a dejected look would spread across my mother's face, conveying what we later learned was a deep sense of paralysis she suffered in the wake of his verbal abuse. Dinner conversation would follow, occasionally peppered with sexist or racist talk, jokes, or stories—all inappropriate for children.

My grandparents, who lived practically next door, were set in their ways. Grandma would cook delicious meals, play Yahtzee and other games with us, and engage us in crafts, always happy to have us around. Grandpa was a salt-of-the-earth guy. Regimented in his routines, every day he wore the same "uniform" for working in the greenhouse—an olive green shirt and pants with suspenders. On occasion, Grandma displayed a self-righteous attitude that led to fights with my dad, after which my siblings and I were not allowed to visit until my father gave us the go-ahead.

Although only twenty miles from Cleveland, we lived like hicks in the boonies. We had a big old country barn that looked like it was about to fall down, as well as lots of chickens, goats, mousing cats, and farm hounds. We hunted rabbits and trapped muskrats in the back fields and ditches. We drank and bathed in well water, even though a fire hydrant across the street provided access to city water. In the heat of summer, we wore overalls with nothing underneath; and the soles of our feet were so tough we could dash barefoot across the gravel driveway.

Conversely, conservative appearance was a must at the bar my father owned and operated in town. There he sported a buttoned-up shirt and trousers, and my mother wore a dress. When we siblings went to the bar, we made sure to dress in nice, simple clothes, usually corduroy or plaid slacks for the boys and a dress for Ruth. Often we had not bathed, since we would get dirty anyway while performing our assigned jobs, such as stocking supplies, sweeping, and emptying garbage. One of the nastiest chores involved going through the week's trash to extract the pieces of aluminum foil in which burgers had been wrapped. My father would then ball up and flatten the mounds of aluminum foil to sell as scrap metal, worth only pennies after the demeaning work of sorting, for which we were not paid. By contrast, my grandfather paid us when we helped out in his greenhouse.

We also wore simple clothes to school—never designer brands like Levi's, Calvin Klein, or even Haines, only off-the-rack items from local discount stores like Hills, G.C. Murphy, Gaylords, Big Wheel, and Gold Circle. Several of my classmates knew I wore discount apparel, which did not bother me.

At the time, small-town Avon was a conservative stronghold. Protesting, had it occurred there, would have been considered un-American. To my father, the only thing more un-American was what he called "those goddamn hippies with their long hair," and so for years we three kids got "bowl" haircuts at the local barbershop. I did not think much about my short hair until high school, when I felt miserable not only about the length of my hair but about having no hairstyle. When in my sophomore year I dared to feather my hair back one day, my father yelled that I looked like "a goddamn fag" and he would take me straight to the barbershop if I didn't fix it. So I began combing my hair down at home and feathering it after leaving for school.

Since there were no computers or cell phones, my only means of escape at home were board games and television with my siblings. At my grandparents' house, there was much more to do and a variety of books to read. Although longing to be cool like the Fonz, I was dorky and, more than anything else, enjoyed reading my grandparents' latest edition of *The Guinness Book of World Records* cover to cover, comparing the statistics cited in it with those of previous years. I also liked poring over a slightly outdated set of encyclopedias, especially to augment schoolwork. I remember being envious of the nerdy kid in an Encyclopedia Britannica commercial, wishing that I, like him, would someday be admitted to Harvard after purchasing a brand-new set of these volumes.

My siblings and I relied on one another, even when we fought. Once, after Bret and I had been arguing, I slammed him into the door leading to the steps upstairs, breaking its wood panels. Fearing our father's rage upon seeing the damage, we were greatly relieved when he came home drunk that evening, stumbled up to his room, and passed out. By the time Dad discovered the broken door, Bret had conjured up a clever explanation for it: Dad, after coming home drunk, had slammed him into the door. Accepting the alibi, Dad told Bret he had better "fucking listen next time." In addition to watching out for each other, Bret and I shared the belief that we were witnessing normal behavior for a father.

Admittedly, for the first eight years of my life, I assumed our entire home situation in Avon was normal. Moreover, I respected my father; in fact, I idolized him, viewing him as a successful business owner, volunteer firefighter, and part-time farmer with over two hundred peach trees. Polite and obedient, I tried to be the best son possible, unaware that my admiration for him would soon be used as kindling to destroy my childhood.

During what was to become my nearly ten years of sexual violation at the hands of my parents, and for decades after, I continued to admire and respect my father. I even wanted to take over his bar when he retired, take charge of farming his land, and be a firefighter like him. Though I did become a firefighter—unlike Ruth and Bret, who continued working at the bar, tyrannized by my father's controlling temperament—much later, with the surfacing of my traumatic memories, I questioned the desire to pattern myself after a man who had deeply traumatized me, and concluded that there was something wrong with me for emulating him, that I was damaged and worthless.[1] Only after decades of filtering life through this lens of shame did I discover that wanting to follow in a father's career footsteps is nothing to be ashamed of; it was my father's abuse that I would have to condemn in order to heal.

Chapter 2

I was part of what seemed like a "standard" family—a still-married mother and father, pets, and three meals a day. We had electricity, running water, a rotary phone, a color TV, and the usual household appliances. But that is where the normalcy ended.

Some of my earliest memories are of my parents walking around our small farmhouse fully naked and of my mother wearing only a very short robe that covered little and my dad wearing a pair of dingy tight whities. We children thought nothing of the flagrant nudity at home. Helping my father take off his socks after he returned from work, an unenviable job made more repugnant by having to clean the crud from between his toes while he sat nude on a kitchen chair, his penis inches from my face, was a daily routine, one among a host of aberrant activities.

My parents' bedroom door was always open unless they were sleeping, a frequent occurrence. Even after a full night's sleep, they would often nap for three to four hours in the afternoon, while we were expected to quietly watch TV downstairs. They probably averaged thirteen to fourteen hours a day in that room, which reeked of stale sex and sweat. When the door was open, they would have sex, argue, or do both at the same time, subjecting us to nearly daily displays of sex mixed with megadoses of verbal and physical abuse. One afternoon when I was about five years old, I walked past their bedroom while they were having sex; saw my father on top of my mother, screaming at her; then heard a loud slap across her face. I didn't linger, for fear of becoming the next target of his wrath. Though now aware that my mother had surely contributed to this debacle, in that moment I felt great pain for her.

Other times when my parents' bedroom door was open, my father would call one of us to empty the yellow-stained, smelly pink piss bucket he used instead of the nearby bathroom toilet, finding it easier to roll his 350-pound body onto its side and urinate while in bed. We would carry the bucket to the bathroom gingerly, so as not to splash its contents on our hands; pour the urine into the toilet; and rinse the bucket out in the bathtub. More often, my father would be on the bed reading the newspaper naked, legs spread, one hand behind his head and the other holding the paper, while my mother, also naked, would be between his legs for hours, with his flaccid penis in her mouth. One of them would then call me to their bedroom to respond to a trivial question, like "What happened at school today?" or a request to get my father a glass of Kool-Aid, only to find them in this position. My mother would perform the acts expected of her, even when subjected to one of his signature putdowns, such as "Jesus Christ, stroke that cock," "Come on, suck it," or "Dig at those balls, Ellie." While aware that my father choreographed his life around his penis, I had no idea how wrong these circumstances were.

Another staple in our house was pornography—not just mainstream fare like *Playboy* magazines, of which there were plenty, but also hardcore magazines sold at adult bookstores, which we children first viewed between the ages five and ten. Not only would these magazines be left in plain sight on the kitchen table and elsewhere, but my father would encourage us to look at them, saying things like, "Hey, come check this out" or "See how hairy her pussy is?" I vividly remember paging through an interracial adult magazine during breakfast with him one Sunday and seeing a photo of a white man having sex from behind with a black woman. Nine or ten at the time and familiar with the sexually descriptive narratives accompanying such photos, I asked my father, "Do you think he's fucking her in the ass?" He replied nonchalantly, "He might be," acknowledging his implicit acceptance of such behavior. And while I don't recall seeing child pornography in the house, I have learned from Bret that my father was in a kiddie porn ring at the time with several other men in Avon.

The prevalence of my father's aberrant behaviors may have been partially obscured by his hypocrisy. He used the N-word, and yet he and my mother would swing with African Americans. He criticized the regulars at the bar for drinking alcohol and yet drank incessantly. He also vigorously condemned the sexual aberrations of other people despite being a sexual deviant himself. For instance, he denounced the father of a friend of ours for forbidding his wife to wear underwear so he could throw her on the ground and have sex with her whenever he wanted, including in front of the children, all the while exposing myself and my siblings to sex with my mother.

The abundance of deviant behavior we observed in our younger years permeated the fiber of our being, though at the time we considered the conduct customary.

Seeing our mother suck our father's limp penis was no big deal. Watching our father take a shit with the door open and wash the crack of his ass with a washcloth was routine. Consuming porn over breakfast on Sundays was a family ritual. That we didn't lose our sanity, resort to drugs, or become dysfunctional members of society is a miracle. There were disturbing repercussions, however. Seeing how life revolved around my father and his penis, I concluded that was how life was supposed to be and became fascinated by my penis, masturbating whenever possible, even before I could orgasm. By the time I had become a preteen, I was obsessed with sex.

CHAPTER 3

MY FATHER'S EARLY LIFE SHEDS some light on his character as an adult while I was growing up. According to my grandmother, he was extremely jealous of his younger brother Jack, who, sickly as a child, received the bulk of his parents' attention, though he grew up to be strong, healthy, and a recognized expert in agricultural pesticides. A high school yearbook photograph shows my father as a popular, well-adjusted young man, as well as an accomplished football player. He could have attended his choice of colleges but instead impregnated a thirteen-year-old Avon girl five years his junior, then promptly joined the army and disappeared from town.

The girl stayed behind in Avon, where her classmates threw "medicine balls" at her stomach in gym class to help her get rid of the baby, as she later recalled. She eventually dropped out of high school and moved to Norfolk, Virginia, where my father was stationed. There they married and she gave birth to a daughter, whom they named Bobbi. Nine months later, my grandparents visited and found their first grandchild to be extremely malnourished and mottled with cigarette burns. When confronted about the burns, my father said, merely, "Well, her mother doesn't smoke." Horrified by the implication of his statement, my grandparents took Bobbi home with them, where she subsequently lived until the age of eighteen, although they never officially requested custody of her.

The marriage between Bobbi's mother and my father was short-lived. After it ended, she told my grandparents she would no longer be coming to see Bobbi, visits she had been making several times a week. My father, who now lived in the basement of their house, distanced himself from his parental responsibilities as well, though there is no question in my mind that during this time, he molested her. Bobbi has told me about showering with him and being "penis-high" to him, and that he nicknamed her clitoris her "little bean"—most likely either to cover his tracks should she ever speak of his actions publicly or to prevent her from doing so—akin to how he had told me his abuse of me should be considered "our time" and "nobody else's business." Bobbi is sure that more happened, but her memories are unclear.

After graduating from high school during the final years of the hippie movement, Bobbi became a free spirit. By then my father, estranged from her, had married my mother and produced three more children. I, the middle child, was disgusted with this girl, ten years my senior, especially after hearing from him that she was "fucking niggers" and "hooked on drugs." My mother, never considering her a stepchild, had made a habit of Bobbi-bashing, telling me and my siblings that she was our "evil half-sister" and a "druggie." Because of my parents' animosity toward Bobbi, seeing her at my grandparents' house became awkward, made all the more so by her insistence on insulting my father, which, as a loyal son, caused me to feel disdain for her. Years later, Bobbi shared an anecdote illustrating my parents' neglectful and hostile view of her. She remembered coming to our house as a teenager one Christmas Day and watching us happily opening presents but never receiving one herself, not even from her father.

Bobbi did become addicted to drugs and alcohol, though she has been sober for twenty-one years. Like me, she battles obesity, a common issue in my family. She's on welfare, due to her past addictions, and has run into trouble with the law. Yet she has raised two psychologically well-balanced children, despite the abuse she experienced.

Retrospectively, I view my longtime alienation from Bobbi as a stain on my character. Even in my forties I sided with my father, including after she sold items she'd taken from my grandfather's barn and yelled to the police that my father was a molester—a stance for which I apologized after learning more about her regrettable upbringing and circumstances.

A story about my father in the 1960s helps flesh out this profile of his character. Between his first and second marriages, and after his discharge from the army, he had a child with a young girl from the neighborhood. Because the baby was put up for adoption and had no interest in finding her birth parents, I never met her. Her mother, who eventually moved to California, remained in touch with my father and returned to Avon when her father became ill, at which point I met *her*. I remember being surprised that she looked at my father, hunched over from the weight of his belly, with love and adoration. Fortunately for her, they never ended up together because she wasn't willing to leave the West Coast and he would not leave Avon.

I was initially told that my father impregnated the girl when she was sixteen. The truth, however, is much more distressing: he was twenty-two at the time, and she was twelve. Her family filed statutory rape charges against my father, who spent a couple months in a low-security prison then had the charge expunged from his record, probably through a financial bribe. To this day, neither the police nor the local prosecutor's office can find a record of this crime, though, according to many Avon residents, my father had bragged about having sex with her from the time she was a teenager into her adult life.

Upon learning these details, I had two gnawing concerns. First, I found it unfathomable that he had not been labeled a sexual predator for life, that men could get away with a crime of this magnitude, suffering nothing more than a slap on the wrist. I also suspected I might have one or more siblings somewhere in the world whom I would never meet. So I joined an online DNA ancestry site in the hope of finding them and learning that growing up outside of our incestuous household had helped them develop into well-adjusted adults unburdened by mountains of shame.

Another story revealing insight into my father's character involves my brother Harry, who died in childhood as the result of an accident due to negligence. Harry was my parents' first child, born about a year and a half before Ruth and named after my father's grandfather. Forced to marry my newly pregnant mother, my father lacked parenting skills, a situation evident from the start. He often boasted about never having changed a diaper. If my mother wasn't home and Harry needed a fresh diaper, my father would take him to my grandmother's house for a diaper change.

Shortly after Ruth was born, Harry developed an interest in spending time with my father. One day, two-year-old Harry wanted to stay with my father instead of going with Ruth and my mother to get her hair done by a neighbor, as was their routine at the time. According to the story I was told, Harry stayed behind in the greenhouse with my father, then wandered off and was found shortly thereafter drowned in a ditch—a situation that would have been treated as a family tragedy, with no police charges filed.

However, the truth revealed to Ruth by my mother shortly before she died, was that she had gone to her hair appointment with Ruth in tow and Harry had stayed with my father, who later walked to my grandmother's house for lunch, forgetting about him. My mother returned to find my father and grandmother at the kitchen table and asked, "Where's Harry?" In no time, the race was on to search for him, whereupon his body was discovered in the ditch and the police were called. For years I could hear my father's voice in my head as he sugarcoated the truth about the incident to the police, so much so that when a high school teacher asked my class to name one thing in life we wished we could have, I said, "An older brother" and explained how Harry had drowned—the untruthful version, the only one I knew at the time. Little did I realize that my wish actually referred to retrieving *many* aspects of my life lost to my father's neglect.

After Harry's death, my mother and grandparents became overly protective of Ruth, and later Bret and myself, as well. But my father simply went about his life eliciting sympathy as a poor man who had lost his son—a narcissist's classic lament. No one else suffered like him; no one else could succeed in life like him; and no one else could have sex like him. Everything, in his view, was about him. Even when my mother died thirty years later and people asked him how he was doing, he would reply, "How the fuck do you think I'm doing? My wife just died." Hearing this, despite knowing he had abused her mercilessly and been responsible for their first child's death, I nevertheless continued to idolize him.

Another salient aspect of my father's life during my childhood was that he had a pseudofamily and we knew about it. Strangely, Ruth kept in touch with this family, and when she tried to uncover abuses he might have inflicted on them, she found that, to the contrary, they thought he walked on water. My hunch is that this situation sprang from an affair my father had with a woman named Dody, a mother who lived on a dead-end street in Avon, whose husband was rarely home. My father "visited" her so often that a neighbor joked about him living there. Surely his 1968 blue International pickup truck, with its roof-mounted volunteer firefighter beacon, was anything but inconspicuous.

My father made no effort to hide the affair from my mother, who, despite my parents' open marriage and reputation as swingers, hated both the relationship and Dody. Her anger led to frequent arguments, resulting in my father spending hours each week at Dody's house. To make matters worse, he had no qualms about bringing her children to our house, further irritating my mother.

Their favorable opinion of my father was probably because he gave them money and bought their house for them when it was going into foreclosure. They were most likely destitute, so helping them out financially might have been deemed considerate had our family not been living so meagerly, acquiring nothing extravagant, often restricted to recycled food choices, and getting toys largely from our grandparents.

Why my father's relationship with Dody's children apparently did not involve sexual abuse mystifies me. The only violation I'm aware of occurred one day when he brought the youngest, a girl of about six, to our house and revealed her vagina to me and my siblings to show us some kind of prolapse. We were told to look, which we did, before she quickly covered up. My father carried out this charade of having two families for a decade, then they left town, likely unaware of the torture those years of incessant arguing between my parents had caused my family as we struggled with this covert abuse toward us.

Even more mystifying to me than my father's purported nonsexual relationship with Dody's children is the fact that after his abuse toward me had ended and slipped into the recesses of my subconscious mind, I remained steadfast in my role as obedient son, my adoration for him never wavering until the Brett Kavanaugh hearing nearly thirty-five years later. Although I'm a fairly intelligent man with considerable common sense, only then could I see through my father's façade to the criminal and malicious person he was.

Chapter 4

In addition to my father, the other guilty party in the abuse I experienced was my mother, Eleanor. And while I sympathize with her as a fellow victim of my father's perversions, my wife Karyn does not. I know Karyn is right, and I now feel anger toward my mother; but I still cannot conclusively condemn her, having watched her suffer at the hand of my father, who constantly belittled her and ordered her to behave in aberrant ways.

A year older than him, my mother had a sad life. One of ten children, she was often ignored, her father focusing more on his horses than his children. She was also picked on at school for having a lazy eye and, as a young adult, for losing her mother to cancer. Recently, my father told me that she had been a virgin at age twenty-three—a woman with low self-esteem, just right for the picking by a sexual predator like him.

Nor did the life of this obviously submissive woman improve after marrying my father. I would like to think she enjoyed being our mother; but I don't remember her ever saying she loved us, and, if she did love us, I find her unwillingness to protect us against my father's aggression inexcusable. She could have escaped with us to the home of any one of her five sisters, who would have welcomed us as they were aware of my father's brash treatment of her. I learned, for example, of a day when my mother wanted to attend the funeral of one of her relatives and my father objected; my grandmother nevertheless took her to the services; and my father showed up and dragged her out of the funeral home. Her only reprieve from my father's humiliations seemed to be while interacting with her regular bar customers, who supported her even in the face of his verbal abuse toward her.

I once believed my mother had done penance for her part in my abuse by undergoing two open-heart surgeries to repair a leaky mitral valve, resulting from a bout of rheumatic fever she had suffered in childhood. Her heart issues, which had increased in severity over time, were exacerbated by the lack of air conditioning at home. Our only air conditioner was a window unit in the upstairs bedroom I shared with Bret, where summer temperatures would often climb to triple-digit highs.

My mother's almost playful nature as she abused me in my younger years was disturbing to recall. I remember her performing oral sex on me at around age nine and my penis being small enough for her to take it easily into her mouth. My father would then instruct her to swallow it, and she, in turn, would gag on it to grant his wish. When combined with alcohol, her actions became outright disgusting. One night my parents came home highly intoxicated and woke me up. My mother enthusiastically performed oral sex on me, followed my father's instructions to put my testicles in her mouth, then had intercourse with me. She closed her eyes and appeared to be enjoying the experience, although I don't remember her orgasming. Another time they came home drunk, they decided to measure my penis and Bret's. As they stood laughing, with my mother poised, ruler in hand, I immediately pulled out my penis to be measured. Bret, on the other hand, cried, wanting nothing to do with this cruel charade.

My mother's cheekiness while abusing me vanished after her first open-heart surgery, when I was fourteen. I can still see the fresh scar I observed soon afterward. The operation, combined with bloating from her heart failure and my considerable weight gain, made her uncomfortable; holding her arms up and hands on my chest, she would do everything possible to stop my body from pressing on her. And I, because of her soreness, would waste no time undressing, performing, orgasming, and leaving, unless my father instructed us to do some other act, in which case it would take as long as he wanted regardless of her discomfort.

My mother died in September 1997, the day before the appointment for her third open-heart surgery. I sometimes think she died to escape my father's grasp once and for all. Yet another casualty of my father's rage, she had succumbed, through exposure to lousy living conditions and perpetual physical and mental abuse, to a slower, more painful death than two-year-old Harry. Grief stricken, I cried uncontrollably at her funeral, with no recollection of the abuse I had suffered, indicating that I had by then repressed my memories of it. Her death was to change me in many ways. I began standing up for myself, and, as such, ended an unhappy marriage I had entered into seven years before, fathering three children. I also started drinking more, and, without my mother's presence as a buffer, the confrontations with my father became more frequent and increasingly intense.

Another fifteen years would pass before discovering how harmed I had been by the people biologically primed from the start to protect and comfort me. As each sinister memory surfaced, my brain landscape seemed to revert to its format at the time of the trauma, making me barely able to distinguish the past from the present. At other times, I would tense up and freeze, flooded with shame at having allowed myself to be coerced into an incestuous relationship with both my parents.

CHAPTER 5

WHEN I WAS NINE, I WAS FORCED to have sex. The first time, I was on top of my mother. I clearly recall having an erection and the feeling of being inside her vagina, coached by my father to "pump" my hips but unable to orgasm.

I have long wrestled with this memory of losing my virginity to my mother at age nine. It first became clear to me the night I woke up Karyn to confess to her the sexual abuse I endured as a child and, in the process, remembered how it all began. I was in fourth grade at Avon East Elementary School. Girls, in my mind, had progressed from having cooties to being people of interest whom I had no idea how to deal with. I was a husky kid and had started wearing glasses. I felt as normal and girl-worthy as any of my buddies.

After school and on weekends, I would drive my father's tractors, especially his McCormick-Farmall Cub, around the family property, feeling grown up and proud as I helped with various projects. I was his "big ace"—a title that initially pleased me but soon led to sibling rivalry and ultimately a realization that big ace really meant top slave. Most often, the tractor I drove pulled an antique sprayer for applying insecticide to the peach trees in the orchard behind our house. I wore no respiratory protection; my protective gear consisted solely of a hat, pants, and a long-sleeved jacket bearing the letters

CPO, styled after coats worn by chief petty officers in the navy. When the wind blew the spray toward me, I was to protect my eyes and lungs by ducking my head under my jacket and holding my breath, a challenge in the heat of summer.

Seeing this jacket in my first extended flashback is what lifted the floodgates causing other streaming images of the day to come back to me. I saw how, on the day the sexual abuse began, my father and I, having sprayed the peach trees, had parked the tractor. Our usual routine was to head for the basement, disrobe, throw our dirty clothes on the wash pile, and shower, him first, beneath the piped-in fixture we had next to a sump hole; as I would stand there naked, waiting for my turn to shower, he would barrage me with sex stories, saying, "I banged [so and so]…I fucked the shit out of her." On this day as I was awaiting my turn to shower, he looked down, noticed I had an erection, and chuckled before going upstairs. I, too, looked down and saw my erection, free of pubic hair growth. Then I showered, dressed, and complied with my mother's request to come to their bedroom. They were naked. My father said something like, "Show her your hard-on." I undid my pants and pulled out my little erect penis. My mother giggled and began flicking it around with her finger. He told her, "Stroke it a little, Ellie," whereupon she began stroking and rubbing the head of my penis. After a couple minutes, I was dismissed and went on with my day.

That night I was awakened by my mother as she quietly told me to come with her, making sure not to wake my brother, who was asleep in the bed next to mine. No sooner did I arrive at my parents' bedroom than my father instructed me to take off my pajamas and climb on top of my mother. She then started touching my penis, and immediately it became hard. Once I was awkwardly positioned on top of her, she guided my hips as I stiffly moved forward, not knowing where to put my penis. Following my father's instructions, she guided my hand inside her, then removed it and put my penis inside her. Next, my father placed his hand on my ass and, pushing my hips up and down, told me to pump them, then pressed my pelvis down.

The orgasmless sex continued periodically for quite some time, always accompanied by instructions from my father, such as, "Just keep pumping." My initial memories were of my mother lying still, waiting for it to be over, but in later recollections of those years she was giggling as if the sex were cute, and often closing her eyes and moaning, no doubt imagining herself having sex with someone else. I had many questions: Why would I have erections? Was something wrong with me? Why would my father instruct me to have sex with my mother? Was this something families generally did? What if people found out? Despite my concerns, I managed to continue with school and my other activities. I also began masturbating without orgasms, curious more about my erections than what orgasms would be like.

As time went on, the sex sessions began to vary. Sometimes my mother would be on top and told to put my penis in her mouth or to stroke my penis and my father's at the same time. I remember how small my penis felt in her mouth and in her hands as she would rub its head with her thumb. Once when she was stroking my penis, juices started coming out. As she rubbed the secretions on the head of my penis, she explained that it was pre-cum and called "thrills," implying that she was willing to continue. After that, ejaculating became a new fascination for me in my solitary orgasmless masturbation sessions.

Such abuse continued on a regular basis. Usually the sessions would start with my mother coming to my bedroom and saying, "Do you wanna?" I suspected it was something she was told to ask and, rather than a question, an announcement of a duty I was expected to perform.

My suspicion proved to be accurate at Easter around my tenth birthday. We typically spent Easter with my maternal grandparents, either at their home in Kankakee, Illinois, or at a resort hotel they would take us to for dinner, swimming, and an overnight stay—a rare nice time. The Easter just after I turned ten we had finished dinner and, after changing into our swimsuits in my parents' room, I was told to stay behind while Ruth and Bret went to the pool. Having been trained for roughly a year, with no prompting I took off my swimsuit and got ready for sex. This time I was on top of my mother. My father, having positioned himself between our legs, watched the action as I pumped away. Suddenly I had a feeling that was simultaneously excruciating and euphoric. Thinking either I had done something wrong or something was wrong with me, I nervously climbed off my mother. My father looked intently at her vagina then voiced a congratulatory "You came." It was my first orgasm. Though I was not sure what had happened, I had the distinct sense of having accomplished a goal he had apparently set for me. Not until I found time alone the next day did I masturbate and, seeing the semen come out of my penis, finally understand what had happened. I needed to process this memory later, along with the correlation between orgasm and shame that was to plague me for years afterward. I came to view it as the origin for all my later shame—regarding orgasms, the abuse, my weight, my insecurities about the opposite sex, my appearance, and anything else that can make a kid feel like a social pariah.

In another flashback portraying sex as a duty I was to perform, I recalled my father driving our family to Illinois the night before the following Easter. While traveling along the dark and desolate turnpike, with the three children asleep in the back seat, I was awakened by my mother and told to crawl up front with my blanket. The blanket was subsequently used to cover me as my mother stroked my penis; there was no need to cover my father's penis, which she was stroking at the same time, because we were all accustomed to seeing it. I was then told to "play with her pussy," which consisted of me putting a finger in her vagina after first applying KY jelly to both. Eventually my father told my mother to start fucking me, whereupon she hiked up her skirt and slid her behind toward me. Holding my penis as I turned toward her, I struggled to enter her but could not, due to its small size. In time we gave up, and I was permitted to return to the back seat.

I was expected to perform sexual acts for my father's benefit in other settings as well, such as the living room, with Ruth and Bret watching television just yards away, and the bedroom I shared with Bret, graced with the only window air conditioner in the house. One sweltering summer day when our beds had been pushed together for my parents' afternoon nap, I was summoned to come enjoy the air conditioning. So I went upstairs, undressed, climbed in bed next to my mother, and lay there for quite a while with my penis erect as they napped. When they woke up, I performed sex, after which my mother stroked my father's penis for several minutes, as instructed. Then, while I was on my side, she moved her vagina over and put my penis inside her. I recall feeling the air conditioning blowing on my back and seeing the eager look on my father's face as she and I performed in this new position. Next, as was customary regardless of the position we were in, my mother would put my penis inside her and, even more disturbingly, would squeeze my penis firmly, as if to discharge every bit of semen into her vagina, then press it closed with her hand until my father put his penis in her.

Another setting my father used for these sex acts was his office at the bar. On mornings when I cleaned the bar with my parents, my mother and I would bring the empty brand-labeled liquor bottles back to the kitchen, where my father would fill them with the cheapest possible low-quality rot-gut whiskey and label them "Whiskey of the Day." Then at the end of the day he would urge me to finish cleaning as soon as possible so I could be "rewarded." When finished, I would go to his office, where, while counting money at his desk with his pants undone, he would instruct my mother to molest me, saying, "Why don't you ride him, Ellie." Since by then it was close to opening time, we would not get fully nude; instead, I would lower my pants, lie back on the rusted frame bed against the wall, with its sweat- and semen-stained mattress free of sheets, and she would take off her underwear, lie on top of me, and follow my father's instruction to lift up her skirt, enabling him to see the show, which lasted either until I orgasmed or a customer showed up. I can still smell the stale smoke and sex that infused the office of that lifelong criminal. Although the smell of smoke that permeated the bar never bothered me, just one whiff of the office had me swelling with shame.

Chapter 6

My father's dog and pony show continued unabated a few days a week over the coming years, amounting to hundreds of such scenarios during my childhood. Most often they began with my mother coming to my bedroom door asking, "Do you wanna?" after which I would go to their bedroom, undress, perform—usually complete with an erection and orgasm—then get dressed and leave. My siblings, meanwhile, would be either asleep in bed, at my grandparents' or a friend's house, or off at a sporting event.

Upon arriving in my parents' bedroom, I would notice my mother looking as if she wanted to get things over with. My father, on the other hand, would be eagerly waiting at the foot of the bed for his private pornography show to begin. Mother would then take a tube of lubrication out of her nightstand drawer and put some on her vagina to assist with arousal. During sex, she never made eye contact with me, and there was no kissing, except once, and no passion—just straightforward sex. As a boy with raging hormones, it felt good to be inside a vagina and to orgasm. Everything else about these sessions disturbed me, and I did my best to separate them from the rest of my life. I'd fill myself with food, focus on school or sports, or, most often, dissociate by getting lost in television.

The sessions that upset me the most were those without orgasm. When my mother was told to put my penis in her mouth, her actions were mechanical. She would look off to the side then move my penis in and out of her mouth. She never kissed or licked it in a sexual manner. Nor did she talk, unlike my father, who would utter obscenities like "You have a big cock for someone your age" or "Suck his balls, Ellie," after which she would comply. To the best of my recollection, I never orgasmed while my penis was in her mouth, which usually constituted a brief prelude to my father's main show of intercourse. With my penis in her mouth I would feel very small and insecure, as if I were doing an unsatisfactory job for him. Another prelude entailed my mother stroking my penis for my father's viewing pleasure or sitting between me and my father, stroking both our penises—something he had probably seen in a porn movie. Rarely did I orgasm at these times, like I did when he directed his show from start to finish. His praise is what I lived for.

When instructed to have sex with my mother, I was most often on top of her in the missionary position. Initially, I had no recall of being in her from behind, in the doggy position, but memories of doing so eventually surfaced. Never, however, did I have anal sex. In our second most frequent position, she would be lying on top of me, and my father would be leaning over the foot of the bed, inches from my penis, watching. At first I didn't know what to do with my hands, so I would place them by my sides till receiving my father's instructions telling me, for instance, to grab her ass and spread her cheeks apart—surely to improve his view. Occasionally, I would touch her breasts, fascinated by them; but she would give me a look, as if saying, "Can't we just get this done with?" after which I would move my hands back to my sides and finish.

Each session's positioning, prearranged by my father, was demonstrated by my mother. If she lay in bed applying lubricant, I knew I was to be on top. If she stood to the side of the bed applying lubricant, I knew I was to be beneath her. If she lubricated then knelt down and leaned over, I knew I was to penetrate her from behind. Whichever position I was in, after I orgasmed, she would squeeze her fingers around my penis as if trying to get every bit of semen into her, then hold her hand there until my father entered her, at which point I would get dressed and leave. He seemed to need the catalyst of a semen-filled vagina to get his usually flaccid penis erect.

His semen fetish showed up in multiple variations. I remember coming home one day, being coached to tell my mother three things I was going to do to her, then sitting next to her on the bed, fully clothed, and saying, as I counted off the items on my fingers: "I am going to eat your pussy, come in your mouth, and fuck you in the ass." To the best of my recollection, none of these actions occurred. Instead, I remember undressing, letting her put my penis in her mouth, holding her vagina open with my finger—all of which I managed to do with no difficulty—and hearing my father tell me, "Eat that pussy," which I could not do. I was then told to have sex with her, my father following after I orgasmed.

Another time, I was made to watch my father perform oral sex on my mother, probably for instructional purposes. I have a clear memory of my face being between her legs and, with my fingers holding her labia open, looking at her vagina while he coached me on the location of the clitoris and how clitoral stimulation made a woman orgasm. I was then encouraged to perform oral sex on her, but I resisted because I couldn't get past the unfresh smell and the massive amount of pubic hair—something my father loved, often pointing out "hairy pussies" in magazines. Eventually, I was told to start pumping, a more likely way for him to get his show.

One night when I was about eleven, I was awakened by my mother and taken naked, except for a towel, to the pool. In the darkness, I climbed the ladder to the deck, removed my towel, and went skinny dipping with my parents. I remember my father cruelly dunking my mother's head underwater and laughing as she came up gasping. Having never before been in the pool without a swimsuit, I remember feeling stimulated by the water swirling around my penis. After a while, my father had my mother sit on the ladder leading to the deck and instructed me to "get up there and fuck her." I remember the sensation of cool water around my erect penis as I entered her warm vagina. We soon wrapped up in towels and went to complete the show so he could watch it in a lighted bedroom.

My felonious parents even found a way to ruin my time at my grandparents' house. While visiting my grandparents with my siblings, I would occasionally be summoned home to do a "chore." Images have come back of me taking a shortcut by jumping the neighbor's fence and of running entirely around it only to find my parents naked in their bedroom, asking me to shut the door behind me and come have sex. Most often when only my parents and I were present, our home became a nudist house in which I was expected to walk through the rooms naked with them until my father decided where and what type of sex was to be performed.

On other occasions, my father and I would take truckloads of geraniums from my grandfather's greenhouse to a business in Kent, Ohio. There we would unload the plants and have a late dinner with the owners. The rides out and back were generally suffused with my father's tales of sexual conquests. I would get worked up, rubbing my penis through my pants, and be ready to perform by the time we returned home.

A more nuanced though equally insidious variation on my father's sex schemes entailed using his other woman, Dody, as an accomplice. She would say to me, with a smile, "Do you wanna?"—the question my mother used for initiating sex acts—obviously informed by my father so he could watch and so I would be embarrassed when approached. One afternoon she asked me this question at the Avon Little League field in front of friends, who wanted to know what she meant. I answered that I had no idea, but my flushed face clearly revealed that I was ashamed, sweating, and distressed. Despite her obvious promptings from my father, I do not recall ever engaging in sex with Dody. The closest thing to it occurred one morning when my father showed me her breasts, emphasizing how dark her nipples were, as she was Native American. He then instructed me to kiss her nipples and suck on them. I am quite sure this is where the interaction ended, if only because her children were asleep nearby. In any case, both Dody's use of that charged question and my father's insistence that I focus on her breasts were indelibly etched, alongside flashbacks of my mother, in my cascade of awakened abuse memories.

Chapter 7

When I was eleven or twelve, we got our first VCR, which turned out to be a mixed blessing. It gave Ruth, Bret, and me a new means of escape from our dismal lives, but also allowed my parents to view porn movies, to which we were privy. In addition, it enabled me to watch them independently and masturbate, which I did frequently.

Before the VCR, our only relief from the tedium of home life came from playing board games, watching one of our three local TV channels, or going to our grandparents' house to listen to their small selection of vinyl records, practically wearing out such albums as ELO's "Out of the Blue," Meatloaf's "Bat Out of Hell," the *Saturday Night Fever* soundtrack, and Fleetwood Mac's "Rumors." The TV classics we watched most on the VCR were *Happy Days, Welcome Back Kotter, The Love Boat,* and *Emergency!,* which undoubtedly helped guide me to my career with the fire service. While watching episodes about Squad 51, I was always excited to hear alarms ring, because it would mean a structure fire and Engine 51 would soon be on the scene, with Captain Stanley, Stoker, Lopez, and the comical Chet Kelly. We also watched classic comedies like *The Blues Brothers, Animal House,* and *Caddyshack*; Bruce Lee karate films such as *Enter the Dragon*; action movies like *The Warriors*; and romantic comedies.

Such escapes into movies made me long for romantic love. I remember having sex at about age ten while on top of my mother; noticing that her eyes were closed and she was moaning pleasurably, as if thinking of someone else; and kissing her in a way my young mind construed as passionate. She shook off my kiss and looked at me as if I were crazy. The shame triggered within me by this scene of myself as a prepubescent child being forced to have sex then being dismissed for my attempt at passion was devastating, so much so that weeks passed before I could share it with Karyn, who knew I had been grappling with something onerous. As it turned out, the shame aroused by this flashback amplified the humiliation I felt after orgasming in my adult life, fearing I would be shunned for attempting to passionately kiss someone I loved and being made to feel I had caused the abuse, or even invited it.

The porn movies my parents watched on the VCR provided something else entirely. After viewing a few of them, my father would use me to help act out scenarios he had seen performed. One day, for instance, he instructed my mother to sit between us and stroke both our penises. Another time he had her kneeling, stroking our penises, then alternately taking each one in her mouth, mine erect and his flaccid until it expanded and stiffened.

I recall two porn movies I had to watch with my parents as a fourteen- and fifteen-year-old. One, called *Taboo* and produced in 1980, was about a woman who had an affair with her son; while watching the scenes unfold, my mother and I were instructed to act out the various sexual positions portrayed. The second movie, released the previous year, was *Love You*, starring Annette Haven. I remember not enjoying its attempt to be artistic—something my father didn't appreciate either, except for the last scene. Here, Annette Haven, squatting beside two men on their backs, put both their penises in her vagina at the same time, which, for my father, was quite a spectacle. After seeing this movie together, my father had me lie on my back beside him then pushed his surprisingly erect penis against mine so my mother could insert them simultaneously into her vagina. Originally we tried this maneuver on my parents' waterbed, but my mother was unable to stay balanced there, so we attempted it on the floor, implementing what was to become, for me, the most disturbing of all our molestation scenarios.

An adaptation of this scenario occurred, too. One day when I was fourteen I got sick at school, which rarely happened, and I remember my mother picking me up, dropping me off at home, then returning to work at the bar. After sleeping for several hours, I was awakened and, feeling better, asked if I wanted to join my parents in their bedroom. When I got there, my mother had my father's penis in her mouth. While I undressed, she applied lubrication to her vagina, climbed on top of him, and inserted his penis in her vagina. Already familiar with this sex act, I needed no instructions as I went behind them and put my penis inside her too. It turns out, based on later memories and my father's candid talk about it, this adaptation of the scenario inspired by *Love You*—with my father on the bottom, my mother on top, and me (or him) behind, pushing both penises into her vagina—may have taken place at least a half dozen times. In an audio recording I later made of him proudly discussing this position, he said that my mother liked it because "it felt like one big cock," and having another penis against his was a turn-on for him as well.

Most of the time we performed this adaptation I was behind my mother, as I can remember trying to jam my small penis inside her without causing my father's to fall out, a maneuver I accomplished by thrusting my hips forward while pushing down on the shaft of my penis, causing me extreme discomfort. Equally distressing, the head of his penis continually rubbed against the underside of mine, producing irritation and redness. The pleasure was all for him. He would orgasm over my penis; then, after finishing, he would instruct me to get on top and he'd watch until I finished, proudly calling it "sloppy seconds."

During later flashbacks about this sex act, I recalled that my mother would at first reach behind to guide my penis into her vagina, but then my father's would fall out, so instead I began putting my penis into her myself and holding it in place. If my father's penis then fell out, which it occasionally did, I would pull out, he would lower his knees, and my mother would hike herself up, grab his penis, and put it back inside her, after which I would reinsert mine. Aggravated by such disruptions, my father subsequently told me to put his penis back inside her, which I began doing before reinserting my penis—a practice which became so routine that I now have the horrific memory not only of feeling his penis touch mine but also of holding his penis in my hand. Fortunately, I do not recall ever having oral or anal sex with him.

Two years after the flashbacks began, while using a photocopier at the fire station, I had a flashback about an adult movie titled *8 to 4*, in which two people have sex on a copier. An X-rated version of the Dolly Parton movie *9 to 5*, it, like *Love You*, starred Annette Haven, one of my father's favorite adult movie stars. I recalled how he wanted my mother and me to act out the entire movie and told me to refrain from orgasming till the end, a tall order for a teenager with raging hormones. As a result, although I hadn't seen this movie in forty years, I could picture every sexual position in it. At one point, I was inside my mother from behind while she performed oral sex on my father. Then she sat on top of me, facing away from him, but he couldn't see, so he had me back into a corner of the couch and, as my mother sat awkwardly on my penis, her legs folded underneath her to mimic a lesbian scene, told me to "eat her out." I, in turn, knelt on the floor and, while watching the movie, used my fingers to stimulate her, refraining from oral sex. To perform the scene with the copier, in which a male actor held the leg of an actress up so the camera could capture the action, I held my mother's leg up to help my father see the performance. Finally, I finished from behind my mother, after which she climbed on top of my father so he could finish. I have no idea where my siblings were while we acted out the entire film, but I do know that because of the explicit sex scenes I was instructed to perform during its long, painful sequence of scenes, this experience stands out as one of my most vivid and gruesome encounters with porn movies in our household.

Discovering the reenactment of pornographic movie scenes in my parents' devious acts caused me to feel deeply dishonored and worthless. Months passed before I was able to separate my parents' abuse from the simulated sex acts in the movies we watched.

Chapter 8

In my preteen years, I tried to maintain as normal a life as possible. All the while, I had to confront issues associated with the ongoing sexual abuse, including an eating problem leading to self-loathing, a devaluation of women, and an inability to stand up to authority figures.

By age eleven, my eating problem was apparent. I remember my mother buying me pants labeled "Husky" while Bret's pants weren't, often giving him ammunition to use against me. Also, I played middle school football but was not in good shape. For one thing, my father was a "clean your plate" fanatic with a weight problem of his own, and I was an obedient son. For another, eating had become habitual. When the abuse began, I sought refuge from my parents' demands anywhere I could—at my grandparents' house, watching movies on the VCR, listening to music—and all the while eating. I would binge eat and snack throughout the day, even when I wasn't hungry. As I progressed from husky to pudgy to fat, I became a target for bullying at school. Ruth succeeded in staving off some of these confrontations, but the attacks intensified, as did my embarrassment and humiliation. I repressed what I could and fortunately never had suicidal thoughts. I did, however, welcome the familiar knock at my door and my mother's inviting "Do you wanna?"

Acknowledging that at such times I was a willing participant in my sexual abuse is among the hardest dynamics

I have struggled with. Priding myself on knowing right from wrong and striving always to do the right thing, I felt pathetic and deeply ashamed with each recollection of these events. Psychologists eventually helped me realize that at the time of the abuse I was just a kid, that it felt good physiologically and temporarily relieved me of the bullying, and that it did not define me. At the time, however, I lacked the desire to improve my situation. So I did nothing to end the regular visits to my parents' bedroom to perform sex acts and, as a result, felt increasingly worthless. Nor did I do anything to stop overeating. In fact, only in the past two years have I managed, with Karyn's help, to begin losing weight through diet and exercise.

My opinion of women in my preteen years suffered greatly as a result of the sexual abuse I sustained. I objectified women, seeing them primarily as sexual accessories and devices for orgasming. Even so, I worshiped women, longing for their love and affection. I adored romance movies and yearned to be the person who found love in the final scenes, like Samantha ending up with Jake in *Sixteen Candles* or Lloyd flying away with Diane at the conclusion of *Say Anything*. The older I got and the more I distanced myself from my father, the more my sexist views diminished. Even so, I retained some sexist traits and did not fully respect women until I had my daughter and met Karyn, who initially showed me how some of my behavior and beliefs could still be construed as sexist. At such times she would call me "Frank Root Jr.," my father's name, to which I would take offense before finally changing my perspective.

My unwillingness to question authority figures as a preteen was just as tenacious, and a soul-crushing way to live. Regardless of how unreasonable my father's requests were—or those of teachers, school principals, and other adults—I automatically deferred to them, much as a brainwashed individual blindly follows the tenets of a religious fanatic or dictator, regardless of the personal costs involved. The costs to community are equally grave: the widespread aversion to challenging authority is how Nazis rose to power and how pedophile priests propagated the centuries'-long abuse of Catholic boys. In my case, the abuse whose imprints I attempted to normalize as a preteen both emerged from and revitalized my inability to stand up to my parents when they asked me to participate in their sex acts—a vicious cycle that took all my strength to later break.

At the time, I was a mere shadow of the person I am now, more like my father's puppet than a human being. I was vulnerable, susceptible not only to his manipulation and coercion but to my own feelings of self-hatred. Breaking free of his authoritarian dictates and prying myself away from his controlling grip—necessary precursors to disengage from the ravenous abuse—did not come easily. It was a slow crawl over decades to finally becoming my own man.

CHAPTER 9

WHEN I WAS FIFTEEN, AN UNUSUAL ACT of molestation at home changed my perspective enough to eventually empower me to stop the sexual abuse. On this occasion, I was home alone when my parents showed up with their friend Lynn, a very attractive lady probably in her mid-thirties, after dropping her husband off at their house. The threesome, intoxicated, were telling stories and laughing together when the woman suddenly stood up, took my hand, and led me to my bedroom. We began kissing and took off our clothes. She lay on the bed, and I performed oral sex on her—to orgasm, I believe. I then entered her vagina and, being well trained, lasted through multiple positions for quite some time before orgasming inside her. Predictably, my father watched the entire encounter through the curtains, as he told me later. She then gathered her clothes and went to my parents' room for sex acts choreographed by my father, having been inspired, no doubt, by his fetish for penetrating a woman with semen in her vagina.

In a strange way, the event boosted my self-confidence significantly. In fact, my experience of a woman in her mid-thirties wanting to have sex with me had so altered my perception of myself that I never imagined the rendezvous had been set up by my father or that she was in fact guilty of child abuse and statutory rape—only that she had found me desirable. In my mind, my physical stature, long portraying me as a social pariah, had suddenly made me attractive to girls. Rebelling, I traded my mandatory bowl cut for a classier hairstyle and soon had girlfriends, though I doubt I ever again had sex with someone other than my mother until after age sixteen.

Infused with self-confidence, I also started standing up to my parents. While the routine of my mother knocking on my door and asking, "Do you wanna?" continued partway into my junior year of high school, I then began providing a new answer to her question. Rather than getting up and traipsing into their room for sex, I would reply, "No," and go back to sleep or watch TV. Invariably my mother would reappear minutes later and ask, no doubt following instructions from my father, "Are you sure?" "Yes, I'm sure," I would respond, astonished that I actually could escape his control.

Only a few times that year did I relent—always after her third request, which went something like "Would you please just come?" My sympathetic nature would win out, and I'd go perform sex. Once, before reaching my parents' bedroom, I heard my father say, disappointedly, "I don't know what the big fucking deal is," then saw him smile upon discovering that I'd arrived, the catalyst he no doubt needed to get an erection. After these few times of giving in to my parents' demands for sex acts, I could feel my self-esteem plummet, a perception that finally fueled the cessation of these visits to their bedroom.

My staunch refusal to submit to my parents' sexual abuse changed the course of my life. I sometimes wonder what would have happened had the sex acts continued. Would I have succumbed to depression, alcoholism, drug abuse, or perhaps committed suicide, like others who have been led down such paths?

Fortunately, the opposite occurred: my life improved dramatically. In my junior year, I went from adolescence to young manhood. Female friends no longer looked at me and my male classmates as the geeky, squeaky-voiced kids we had been the year before. I made the varsity football team. I also mustered the courage to run for class president—and won. The following year I was elected senior class president without opposition, a feat in which I took great pride. Also that year I made the honorable mention conference for football; was named field event captain for the track team; and was declared "student with the most school spirit, most involved in school, and biggest flirt." I had girlfriends, but no long-term relationships and few sexual encounters, due both to the innocence of the times and my refusal to force anyone into acts that had been foisted upon me.

Meanwhile, I spent the rest of that year, as well as my senior year of high school, sustaining direct confrontations with my father. For example, angry that the time required of me as class president infringed on the slave labor he expected of me at his bar and at home, he ordered me to quit my position at school, which I refused to do. I managed to withstand other crises, too, —like growing my hair out, listening to rock 'n' roll, and staying out past 9:00 p.m. with classmates—thanks to the help of my siblings and good friends. I also enjoyed sleepovers at friends' houses, although no one was ever welcome to spend the night at my house. Undaunted, I realized that as liberating as it had been to have stood up to my father's sexual abuse, I had to muster yet more strength to free myself from his control over other aspects of my life.

CHAPTER 10

AFTER HIGH SCHOOL, MY FATHER wanted me to go to college and play football. Though the idea appealed to me, there was no course of study I wanted to pursue. All my life I had yearned only to be a firefighter, which did not require a college education. My discussion with my father about bypassing college did not go well. He argued, "What the fuck will you do with your life? Are you going to be a fucking bum?" When I finally told him I wanted to be a firefighter, he said, "Okay," but offered no apology for his derogatory questions.

When I was eighteen and just out of high school, a civil service entrance exam for firefighter/EMT was being given in Avon. I signed up for it and, in September 1984, after scoring well, was made a volunteer firefighter with the local fire department. Fortunately, the exam did not include a lie detector test; if it had, and if I had answered no to a question about ever being involved in sexually deviant activity, my reply would have registered as deceptive and made me ineligible for a job.

The fact that I did not leave home at eighteen despite being free of the sex demands reflects the degree to which I still felt ruled by my father. And indeed, as a volunteer firefighter, I felt him controlling aspects of my occupation, all the more so after he was declared fire chief in 1988 and became my boss. One of my father's last digs at me as his employee came years later, in 2001, while the fire station was under construction. I had been appointed to the committee overseeing the project and was suddenly dismissed for not concurring with the design my father wanted; he had proposed a one-story station appearing as if it had a second floor, with lots of wasted space, while I had recommended a two-story station. Unfortunately, his need to still control me resulted in the city's taxpayers getting a building that our personnel outgrew within ten years.

Happily, to stave off my father's attempts to control me, I had by then accepted a job as a full-time firefighter in Elyria, a larger city southwest of Avon. The training for this full-time position had been comprehensive. I had taken every class I could in fire inspection, fire instruction, command, and paramedic training. Bringing these enriched perspectives to my ongoing work at the Avon Fire Department helped me oversee its development from an inadequate facility to a well-equipped and highly operational one. It also changed the dynamic between my father and myself, creating friction that sometimes had me nearly shouting at him—a far cry from the behavior of the subservient boy constantly padding off to his parents' bedroom on command.

For seventeen years, I was employed in both departments, working up to lieutenant in Elyria and captain in Avon, and becoming a fire command instructor equipped with skills, knowledge, and experience that far exceeded my father's. Surpassing his level of expertise in every aspect of the fire service, I regarded him as nothing more than a figurehead who got what he wanted at work because of his seniority. I now had to decide which department to stay in, because the Avon Fire Department was transitioning to full-time service and I couldn't do both. Having been pivotal in its growth and expansion, I opted to stay with this station. The only downside was a few more years of grappling with my father, a vastly underqualified full-time fire chief, as my primary employer. Finally, in 2006, the servant became the master as I was appointed fire chief, officially taking the reins of the Avon Fire Department and at last gaining sovereignty over my career.

CHAPTER 11

IN 2006, MY LIFE BEGAN ANEW in many ways. Following my promotion to fire chief in February, I no longer had to contend with a hostile work environment. My father, while continuing to undercut me, began redirecting his control tactics, calling the mayor to complain about me, getting information on me from one of my crew members, and telling patrons at his bar that I made ridiculous amounts of money. My siblings had it worse. Working there at poverty wages, they were belittled constantly and verbally abused, often in front of his patrons.

That same month, better able to focus on my personal life, I came to realize how deeply rewarding it was to be a father. My children from my first marriage—Kaylee, Frankie, and Evan—had come to accept the divorce as part of their lives and were happy to have "dad time." We'd go to the zoo occasionally, or spend the day at a park. Being the focus of their love and attention meant the world to me. As for my father, they knew him only as a grumpy man good for birthday money and access to a swimming pool, a pond for fishing, lots of land for sports and activities, and cousins living nearby. Although I still lacked recollections of what he had put me through, I never allowed my children to be alone with him, as he had no paternal instincts. That February, with more capacity to attend to my personal life, I pledged to be someone my children could look up to and respect, to avoid acting like an authoritarian figure, and to protect them from engaging with anyone like my father.

In April, I met Karyn, a public health nurse whose eldest son was on the same baseball team as Frankie, my eldest son. When I first saw her sitting on the bleachers, my heart skipped a beat. Soon after getting to know each other, I knew I wanted to spend the rest of my life with her. In July, she and her two boys, Xavier and Alex, joined me and my children to create a blended family that, from the start, has made me happy and proud. Karyn and I got married two years later, in August 2008.

We initially lived in a house I had bought next to my father's, which proved to be an unwise purchase. I had thought that moving there, to the far west side of Avon from where I had been living, would provide continuity for my children following the divorce six years before. Because of my depleted finances, my father had helped me buy the house. And while I assumed he had simply cosigned on the mortgage loan, I was to discover years later that it included a survivorship deed transferring property ownership to him if I were to pass away—yet another of his attempts to assert control over my life. Adding fuel to this inferno, he refused to allow me to add Karyn's name to the deed and mortgage following our marriage, a request I had voiced since she and I had made all the mortgage payments. It finally became clear that my father hated Karyn, although she had cooked him meals, invited him to dinner, and made every effort to be nice to him.

Despite our acrimonious relationship with my father, as years went by, our children did well, with four going to college and one joining the military. We took many family vacations, things I'd never experienced as a child.

The Avon Fire Department flourished, as well. We doubled our staff and acquired new equipment, including Avon's first ladder truck; created a fire prevention bureau; and set up a training division. I took great pride in these accomplishments, all fulfilled against the backdrop of my father's relentless insinuations about my inability to measure up to his standards.

Finally, in April 2021, after nearly thirty-seven years of service, I retired. Not only did I have nothing left to prove in my career with the Avon Fire Department but, more importantly, I was ready to go public with my abusive childhood and refused to involve my co-workers in the ordeal. I assumed that some good friends in the department would support me and others would regard me as the man who fucked his mother, though it turned out that the Avon Fire Department was more supportive than I had expected, though the city and administration were not as forward-thinking. My other main concern about going public was its potential impact on my children. I did not want them ostracized from the community, which could easily have occurred as it had for children in towns where victims of sexual abuse were treated like perpetrators, mental illnesses were stigmatized, and children were judged because of the race, sexual orientation, or behavior of their forebears. I also hoped my children would support me during what was surely to be the toughest chapter of my life as I prepared to reveal publicly and come to terms personally with my history of sexual abuse, much of which I had by then uncovered.

Throughout this turbulent time, Karyn remained my rock and the love of my life, despite the bombshell I had dropped on her. She'd had some moody days, understandably, then invariably came back stronger and more empathetic. With each new revelation of abuse, I'd told her she had every right to move on; yet, amidst her horror, she had not only stayed with me but offered enormous support. We both felt that getting the truth out, receiving therapeutic help, and striving to make my father accountable for his vile behavior would further strengthen our foundation going forward.

CHAPTER 12

Before speaking publicly about my years of child sexual abuse, I had not only uncovered numerous incidents but confirmed some of them with family members. Weeks after breaking my silence to Karyn following the first intrusion of molestation memories, I asked my siblings to share their memories of any sexual abuse they endured as children. At the start, we all agreed that having to see our parents constantly naked and having sex was itself an affront.

The first to acknowledge that something more had occurred was Ruth. When I asked her to be more specific, she said she remembered either walking past our parents' bedroom with the door open or opening the door without knocking, seeing me on top of my mother having sex, and not speaking of it for fear of inciting my father's wrath. I then elaborated on the extent and duration of my sexual encounters with our parents, after which Ruth, stunned, recalled about twenty incidents of sexual abuse by my father, including having to deal with "his limp dick" at around age twelve. She said he would ask her to rate the oral sex he performed on her, probably to see if she was close to orgasming, and that she would wriggle around so much that my mother had to lie on her to hold her still.

When I asked how the abuse stopped, Ruth told me that at age eleven or twelve she was adamant with both our parents that she was no longer going to participate in any of this, demonstrating an enviable degree of self-confidence, but conceded that my father's verbal abuse continued. She also explained that years later he gave her a provocative picture of herself naked as a child, as if giving her a present. Disgusted, she immediately burned the picture. Although she is now beaten down and struggling with alcohol as a direct consequence of his continued verbal abuse, she takes pride in having had the strength and courage as a young lady to stand up to a molester and his accomplice.

Bret, on the other hand, said initially that he had no memory of sex acts occurring between any of us and our parents. I told him of a strong memory I had recaptured of him walking in on me having sex with my mother, with me on top, her on the bottom, and my father watching. I had seen Bret open the bedroom door, look at us in amazement, then promptly pull the door closed. Mortified, I had wanted to stop but my father had said to keep pumping and finish. As we all then went about our day, I was terrified of what Bret might say, but he said nothing. His silence, however, was short-lived. A few days later, while playing baseball behind the bar with the neighborhood kids, he and I began arguing, then Bret shouted at me for all to hear, "At least I don't fuck our mother." I waved at him dismissively, whereupon he yelled, "I saw you fucking Mom." I ran to the bar and told my father that Bret was upsetting me, but lacked the courage to say anything further. Eventually, I returned to the playground, where the game had apparently ended, and as I approached one of the girls to find out why, she looked up at me with an expression of disgust and said, "Did you really fuck your mother?" "No way," I replied, adding that Bret had just been talking shit. Fortunately, the conversation ended there, never to be resumed—after which I repressed all memory of the event, along with many others.

At first, Bret had no recollection of either the bedroom or playground event. Weeks later, however, he reported a vague remembrance of the playground incident, making me think he might still be repressing memories of the sex act he had seen. Despite his ongoing insistence to the contrary and Ruth's agreement with him, regarding him as my mother's "Baby Boy" whom she protected from our father's predatory behaviors, I remain concerned that Bret was molested too. For one thing, he has admitted to me that he does "stuff" some people might consider sexually deviant and wonders if anything in his childhood caused this behavior. He also recalls being in the room when my father took the picture of Ruth naked as a child. In addition, I occasionally wrestle with an unclear memory of Bret, at age twelve, walking into my parents' bedroom and lying awkwardly on top of my mother. I am torn between considering this a true recollection of the event or one I conjured up to avoid thinking of myself as the only son who committed incest.

My siblings and I continue to collectively process memories of the parental abuse we suffered as they arise. When we wonder how we could have stopped it from recurring, we remind ourselves that at the time it took place, we were kids living with our parents, the perpetrators. As such, who could we have turned to? Who would have listened to us? How could we have been brave enough to come forward? Would anyone have acted on our behalf if we had? What repercussions would we have faced? Unfortunately in the 1970s, especially in a small town devoid of resources for us to turn to, our father banked on the fact that shame would keep us from going public, making us all fair game for the perverse acts he choreographed. Now that family secrets have become intrusive memories rudely interrupting our lives, we can at last unravel our experiences and work toward healing.

CHAPTER 13

THE FIRST TIME I SHARED my painful memory fragments of abuse with anyone other than Karyn and my siblings was within the supportive confines of a therapeutic relationship. It was Karyn, who, upon first hearing about my molestation, began looking for a therapist for us. She thought, and I agreed, that I would feel most comfortable with a female who was somewhat older than us and well established in working with adult survivors of child sexual abuse and trauma. We were lucky to quickly find in a nearby community a highly trained and accredited psychologist who met our criteria.

Initially, our sessions with her were emotionally draining. I did the bulk of the talking, chronicling one disgusting detail after another, with the therapist periodically offering reassurances that I was okay, strong, and heroic for having withstood the abuse. Never had she heard of a worse case of it. Listening week after week to accounts of her spouse performing unspeakable acts with his parents took a massive emotional toll on Karyn, however. In retrospect, as much as I wanted her there for support and believe she wanted to be there for me, I'm convinced she should not have been included in my sessions or otherwise subjected to my horrific accounts.

Eventually it became necessary for Karyn to seek counseling of her own and for me to refrain from sharing my flashbacks with her outside of therapy. Curiously, many of these were so vivid and intense that, despite my silence, she could tell by my mood, especially when I'd seem distant or zoned out, that I was reliving my past. In such moments she would console me, and if she asked for information, I would do my best to avoid burdening her with details of the agonizing ordeal.

In time, Karyn's therapist diagnosed her with PTSD. I was devastated to realize that I had caused her so much pain. I felt simultaneously selfish for having relied excessively on her to help sustain my well-being and deeply grateful for her unwavering support while I processed the insidious events of my past. I have since learned healthier ways to take care of myself and emotionally nurture Karyn. Overreliance on a partner, it is now known, often signifies an underlying childhood trauma of abuse.

One weekend soon after Karyn's diagnosis, Ruth, Bret, and I met to discuss how to have our father punished for his crimes. At the meeting, an opportunity for us all to unburden ourselves of painful memories of his abuse, we began collaborating on a plan to make him accountable for his past behavior. We met a second time to explore ways to bring him to justice. The bombardment of memories from my siblings opened a huge pocket of memories in my brain, causing them to stream out as fast as I could talk about them. I now knew I had to act, and I felt emotionally ready to take him down.

Still lacking, however, was the mental fortitude I would need to conduct this mission. To rectify the situation, in December 2019, after a year of attending therapy twice a week, I decided to terminate my sessions and begin functioning on my own, while gradually tapering off of Wellbutrin—an antidepressant I'd been on for three months to help offset lapses in focus and concentration attributed to the abuse revelations. While on Wellbutrin, I had taken a leave of absence from work to recover from my weakened state, rife as it was with depression and episodes of zoning out. Aware that I was not on my A game, I had opted out of work to preserve safety for my fire crews, but I had no idea that the taunting I was to receive from city administrators fixated on their employee's "mental issues" would propel me to engage in self-reflection. The increased self-awareness improved my ability to focus, concentrate at will, and, in general, stop sabotaging my efforts to succeed at work.

The results of my December 2019 mission to become mentally prepared to confront my father were promising—so much so that I returned to work in March 2020 fully confident in my ability to do the job. Coinciding with my return, however, came one of the greatest challenges of my career—the COVID-19 pandemic. The pandemic was unlike any emergency I had dealt with in the fire service; normally, whether responding to a structure fire or mass casualty incident, I was in my wheelhouse, able to keep cool under pressure and direct firefighters to the desired outcome. The pandemic, on the other hand, required nonstop thinking outside the box. Fortunately Karyn, a resourceful public health nurse, helped me make informed decisions each step of the way to improve Avon Fire Department's approaches to everything from patient care to keeping crews in the station as distanced as possible during their twenty-four-hour shifts until vaccinations became available, by which point my stress and anxiety had become palpable.

To gain the mental stability I needed to hold my father accountable for his vile behavior, I knew I had to get back into therapy and find a new therapist. Due to the extra demand for mental health services at the time, I spent months on a waiting list before beginning treatment in a series of remote sessions. The therapist decided early on that, due to my repression, type of abuse, and incapacity to process it as a child, I would benefit from eye movement desensitization and reprocessing (EMDR) therapy—which enhances mental strength by stimulating both sides of the brain while the individual processes traumatic events—a technique in which she was not certified. Fortunately, I soon managed to find a local therapist who was.

My new therapist and I had our first EMDR session after spending countless hours getting to the core of my disturbing childhood memories; exploring the underlying events that had left me feeling flawed, powerless, and worthless; examining how that shame had seeded emotions, behaviors, and relationship dynamics that, while ensuring my survival at the time, impacted negatively on my adult life; and addressing ways to root out the shame. In a pivotal EMDR session early on, I learned to reframe my participation in sex acts with my parents from deeds undertaken out of weakness, having allowed myself to be abused, to deeds undertaken because I was young, obedient, and enjoyed feeling good.

Another important EMDR insight came from comparing photographs of myself as a happy child in third grade with images of myself as progressively more miserable in fourth grade, fifth grade, and sixth grade (see pages 82 and 83). My fourth grade photo, which showed me heavier than before and lacking my earlier sparkle, had long triggered within me debilitating feelings of self-loathing; but after realizing, through EMDR, that the unfortunate image dated back to my earliest experiences of the abuse, I was no longer affected by my altered appearance because I knew it reflected my circumstances, not some deeply ingrained personal flaw.

My therapist also asked to see a picture of my parents and of the three most recent generations of males in my family (see page 84). The image of my parents brought to mind my thoughts of them in general, allowing me to process the love-hate relationship I had with them and how the years of molestation were offset by my desire to be a good son and to earn their approval. I used the picture of me, my father, and my grandfather, taken at the Avon Fire Station, where we all worked, with EMDR to delve into my mind for illumination on what had created the monster who fathered me. Nothing surfaced in memories of my grandfather to explain the demon his son had become. Indeed, I can now concede that, sadly, the origin of my father's evilness may never be known.

EMDR sessions occurred whenever my therapist felt I was ready to confront another disturbing memory. Sometimes weeks passed between sessions since it would take that long to wrestle with a memory, after which I would be mentally exhausted but essentially purged of its emotionally harmful effect on me. Even a single session rich with details, for instance, could spiral from one horrific memory to another, plunging me ever deeper into my mind to uncover the trauma before revealing in five minutes a full hour's worth of work. Though mentally and emotionally spent, I felt that after a year of sessions we had addressed some of the most sickening abuse of my childhood.

When I first started the EMDR sessions, my therapist wanted to know what I'd hoped to accomplish with

In third grade

In fourth grade, when the abuse started

In fifth grade

In sixth grade

My mother and father

Three generations of Frank Roots

therapy. I told her I wanted to uncover all my horrific experiences of the abuse so that the random trickling out of dormant memories would stop. I also explained that if anything of a homosexual nature had happened between me and any other family member, I wanted to know I could deal with it; and indeed, my last few powerful EMDR sessions left me 99 percent sure that no such activity had occurred. In addition, I was hoping to get to the basis of my eating disorder, which, though we found a link between sex, reward, and food, to this day remains only partially resolved.

EMDR soon catalyzed huge developments for me. First, having initially learned to equate sex with love, I gained clarity on this misconception and came to understand sex as a wonderful physical act shared with a consensual partner and love as an all-encompassing feeling for someone who means more to me than life itself. I also acquired insight into my tendency to associate orgasms with shame, a connection dating back to my first experience of orgasm, when I became convinced that I'd done something wrong and disappointed my parents. Just as importantly, I came to accept that I had indeed performed oral sex with my mother, as indicated in haunting flashbacks I'd previously found too abhorrent to acknowledge. In fact, I saw how I had been forced to do it, with my father instructing me and my mother to move into a mutual oral sex position so that, while she was performing oral sex on me, I would use my fingers on her. In a related EMDR session, I recalled being quite young, maybe ten or eleven, when he told us to "69." I lay flat on my back; then she climbed on me, pinned my arms down with her legs, and, using her fingers to open her vagina, lowered it onto my face. With my father coaching me to "eat that pussy," I reluctantly performed oral sex on my mother. My therapist helped me process that horrific memory for several sessions until the thought no longer devastated me. The progress I made in these early EMDR sessions helped me live more comfortably with myself and simultaneously gave me the mental strength and emotional courage I needed to confront my father.

Chapter 14

My siblings, Karyn, and I agreed in October 2018 that it was time to take legal action. Our initial steps led to frustration after online research revealed that Ohio's deadline for filing a lawsuit for child abuse was twenty years—a statute of limitations that, in our case, had already passed. Twenty years didn't seem right to me, considering that I had needed forty years to simply recall memories of the abuse, let alone summon the courage to come forward with them.

Next, Karyn called a high-profile attorney from Cleveland who specialized in child abuse cases. Although he said he would get back to her after discussing our situation with another attorney, he never did—not because nothing could now be done but, I suspect, because the case would not have been lucrative enough for him. He had, after all, been more interested in knowing whether a business or organization had been involved than in learning more about the abuse itself.

In the end, we were blatantly aware that to hire a lawyer we would need proof of the abuse. After exploring a few options, I proposed using my smartphone to record my father commenting on the molestation after I had appealed to his narcissistic appetite to get him to talk about it—a plan we agreed to adopt. For days I pondered how to start the conversation and segue into discussing my age at the time of the abuse. Finally, on Veteran's Day 2018 I waited for him to come home from work then, phone in hand, went to talk to him. Following is a slightly modified transcription of the voice recording of our conversation:

ME: Hey, it's Veteran's Day. Aren't you off today?

DAD: I've never been big on Veteran's Day. All I did was work in a fucking army grocery store. It's not like I got shot at.

ME: Do you get to watch porn anymore?

DAD: I do once in a while, with my girlfriend Aletha. Christ, she's got a bunch of them.

ME: I don't know if you noticed the latest thing online—that double vagina number. What was the name of the porn star we watched who put two dicks inside her?

DAD: Annette Haven. Boy, she was beautiful.

ME: I was thinking Veronica Hart. I'll do a search on that.

DAD: Christ, your mom and I used to fuck that guy Carter. All of a sudden he'd walk up behind her or come in behind her, nail her, and she'd damn near shit herself.

ME: Who was he?

DAD: A guy she fucked for a long time. Boy, could he fuck her too.

ME: Well, we tried it, right?

DAD: Yeah, we did.

ME: Was she able to do it?

DAD: Oh yeah. She told me it just felt like one big cock even if we went at different times. She liked it.

ME: So, how old was I when Lynn, that lady in her mid-thirties, showed up?

DAD: Christ, you weren't old enough to drive, Frank.

ME: I thought I was. I tell everybody that's how I lost my virginity.

DAD: Was it really your first piece of ass, son?

ME [assuming he meant outside of the incest]: Yeah.

DAD: Well, she was a great fuck. Was it just the one time?

ME: Yeah.

DAD: She said you tried another time but she couldn't do it.

ME: She was drunk that day.

DAD: You tried to kiss her, or some goddamn thing. She came into our bedroom, told us she jumped off you, and asked, "God, what do I do?" Eleanor said, "What do you mean?" She answered, "Well, that's your son." Eleanor told her, "Just go ahead and finish him." But she didn't want to make you because you were so fucking good that she thought she'd want more.

ME: Ha-ha, so it must have been right around the time I was starting to drive.

DAD: Yeah. Your mom loved to fuck, didn't she? She also loved to fuck around. Can you believe she was a twenty-three-year-old virgin when we met?

ME: Was she really? Well, do you have any problem with your prostate these days?

DAD: I piss every hour all night long.

ME: When you started having orgasms, did anyone tell you what to expect?

Dad: No.

Me: I'm not sure when I started. All I remember is that I was inside Mom and all of a sudden I didn't know what was going on. You and Mom said, "Oh, you came."

Dad: I know your cock wasn't very big at the time, something you thought would bother her. But she was always willing to fuck you, wasn't she?

Me: Seemed like it. She was always the one who came to get me.

Dad: Yeah, she liked me to fuck her in cum. That was her big thing.

Me: Your cum inside her?

Dad: No, me following a guy in after he came. She loved that.

Me So when I was done, you would . . .

Dad: Yeah. When it was Carter and that black guy Maxwell, I sat back and watched them come so fucking much they'd be plugged in and the cum would run down the crack of her ass.

Me: As for me, I'm guessing I was about eleven.

Dad: You were pretty young. No more than twelve. I don't think you came at first—maybe after two or three times—or many times afterward. If anyone knew, we'd both be in trouble, wouldn't we?

Me: Oh, shit.

Dad: Christ, she'd go to jail, and I'd go to jail.

Me Yeah.

Dad: I have no problem with it. She liked it. You liked it. Christ, how many times do you think you fucked her, Frank?

ME: Oh, probably hundreds over the years.

DAD: You must have fucked her until you were sixteen or seventeen years old.

ME: I want to say it stopped soon after that time with Lynn. That's when I, um, started getting some confidence with girls.

DAD: Your mother didn't have any problem sucking your cock, or anything.

ME: Yeah.

DAD: She loved to fuck. Anytime she wanted some cum in her so we could fuck she'd say, "Hey, I'm going to go get Frank." It was fine with me.

ME: All right.

DAD: Does it bother you now?

ME: I don't know. I was just thinking . . .

Here the discussion turned to a retired local fire chief charged with statutory rape, whom my father had defended in court.

DAD: It's a strange fucking deal with that guy going to jail big time. You never told Karyn about things with your mom?

ME: Oh god, no. Just that I saw two guys and a girl at the same time and remembered that porno. I'll have to look up Annette Haven, eh?

DAD: We did that quite a bit with Carter. Never with Maxwell. Hell of a feeling. We'd fuck a while and then I'd pull out because you'd be rubbing against my side, making me lose control.

Me: Uh-huh, I remember that.
Dad: Okay.

I felt I had played my father for a sucker. Putting him in the spotlight, I had said what he wanted to hear and he sang like a canary, revealing incriminating details because he was not only narcissistic but also dumb. Had I referred to a list of discussion topics, I would surely have learned more details about what had occurred and he would have further incriminated himself. At the time, however, as painful as it had been conversing like this with my father, I was gratified that we now had direct evidence from him about the abuse, including that it had started when I was very young and he, decades later, still found it acceptable.

Chapter 15

With the recording of our father's confessions finalized, my siblings, Karyn, and I reviewed how best to hold him accountable for his actions. We agreed that if child abuse laws had been written to protect victims instead of abusers, our task might already have been complete. But since they hadn't been, we felt it necessary to gather more evidence of his criminality.

Recalling that my father had taken an explicit Polaroid picture of my mother on top of me, with my penis in her vagina, I attempted to locate it. First, I called my father and, speaking softly, as if to keep our discussion private, I told him that Karyn and I weren't having much sex anymore. But before I could get to the point of the call, he offered to hook me up with someone his girlfriend knew, a "gold digger" forty years younger than him. I told him I'd think about it, then asked if he still had the picture of me "fucking my mom." He excitedly told me that he did and would get it for me then and there, but I scheduled it for the next day so I could record the transaction. The next day I called him and, again speaking softly, arranged a time for me to pick up the picture when neither Karyn nor his girlfriend would be present. I wanted to ensure that his girlfriend would not suspect my motives or interfere with the recording.

Following is a condensed transcription of our conversation:

Me: Hey.
Dad [holding the photo]: That's a hell of a shot.
        You have her by the ass.
Me: Yeah.
Dad: Ready to get fucked?
Me: Oh yeah. So, I can keep that picture?
Dad: Yeah. But she ain't giving you much body.
Me: Nah.
Dad: I was a lucky guy.
Me: Oh yeah. You once showed me Dody's tits
        because her nipples were so brown.
Dad: You should see this one's tits—they're
        gorgeous. Did she let me show you?
Me [mindlessly, to keep the discussion going]:
        Yeah, and I think I kissed them.
Dad: I don't remember. She was a great fuck. I got
        excited looking at this yesterday.
Me: Just one picture, huh?
Dad: It's the only one I could find.
Me: I wonder how old I was here.
Dad: Must have been fifteen, sixteen.
Me: I'd say fifteen at the most, because I started
        getting girlfriends then. See, I don't have much
        leg hair there, though my hands look big.
Dad: I wouldn't tell Karyn about this.
Me: Hell no.

I returned home somewhat disappointed. For one thing, I wished I had learned more about Dody to help expand the pool of evidence I'd gathered. For another, asking about more pictures had not led me to my father's photo stash, which I would have liked to search for more incriminating items. Still, I was feeling triumphant about the new evidence I had gathered, some of it graphic and convincing.

Chapter 16

Undeterred by the expiration of Ohio's statute of limitations, my siblings, Karyn, and I decided in early 2019 to move forward with our plan to hold our father legally accountable for the sexual abuse I had endured, since we now had irrefutable proof in hand. We had an audio recording of my father talking candidly about performing sexual acts with me and a Polaroid photo of me and my mother in a sexual act, both attesting to my young age.

In April, Karyn and I consulted our personal attorney about the situation. Saddened by our struggle, he agreed that the statute of limitations was the main obstacle and said he would speak with a prosecutor about our options. In response to his request, we gave him copies of the audio recordings, the photo, and a history of events I had compiled months before. In a follow-up meeting with him at the county prosecutor's office, an assistant prosecutor listened to our saga and reviewed the evidence. Much to our surprise, he stated that we could only charge my father with pandering child pornography for having given me the photo of myself as a minor having sex. We were extremely disappointed that the serial pedophile I had grown up with would get away with more than a decade of child abuse, but felt the pornography charge would at least let people know the kind of monster he was.

The case was to be turned over to local law enforcement, so at my next daily staff meeting with the mayor and the police chief, I gave them a heads up. The police chief, leery of handling a case involving charges filed by the current fire chief against the former fire chief—an issue I silently maintained should not have been problematic—transferred it to the county sheriff's department. The detectives there were preoccupied with a shooting, however, so the police chief tried transferring our case first to an outside private investigator and then to an investigator from the prosecutor's office, neither of which panned out. Next, he reached out to the state's Bureau of Criminal Investigation, also to no avail. All this chaos, in conjunction with constant flashbacks about my sexual abuse, brought me close to a breaking point. Then in September a friend in the Avon Fire Department came into my office as I was staring blankly out the window and advised me to take time off to chill down. That was when I took my three-month leave of absence from the job that had long been my life.

Soon afterward, it was decided that the police department's detective bureau would handle the case, which was then assigned to a detective with no ties to Avon, having recently transferred in from another city. When he reached out to us, Karyn and I gave him copies of the audio recordings, the photo, the list of events, and contact information for my father and the four of us filing the claim. After reviewing the material, he confirmed that pandering child pornography was all that my father could be charged with. He then contacted my siblings, who acknowledged that molestation had occurred in our childhood home and that my father was deeply disturbed. Ruth went on to describe a picture he had taken of her as a young girl sitting on the couch with our intoxicated mother standing naked beside her. The detective explained that unless my father had given it to her, it could not be used as evidence of criminal activity.

Next, he asked my father to come in. My father, it turned out, was shocked to learn the appointment pertained to my complaint and the photo of me in a sexual act as a child. He flippantly stated that the photo showed me and my mother having sex and that all he did was take the picture. The detective did not reveal his awareness of the audio recordings, which contradicted my father's denial of participating in the sexual acts. The detective's report, together with the evidence, was sent to the prosecutor's office, and in November 2019 my father was indicted by a grand jury.

He was required to turn himself in a couple days later. Karyn and I watched from a distance as he entered the police station while a photographer from the local news media took pictures of him. I would like to say I felt joyful seeing him do the perp walk, but I actually felt a little sympathy for him—not because he was my father but because he was now a hunched-over eighty-plus-year-old man who had lost his vibrancy. Hours later, with the charges against him about to be made public, I told members of my fire department, in a speech videoed for posterity, why I had taken a leave of absence. The on-duty crew, whom I addressed directly, was very understanding, but my emotions prevented me from approaching the other two shifts, who instead watched the video.

After being processed at the police station, my father was taken to the Avon Municipal Court for arraignment. There the judge, to whom he had donated funds over the years, released him upon signing a bond after pleading not guilty, even though he had the requisite ten-thousand-dollar cash bond in his pocket. This felt like a bad omen of things to come. Would my father, who had for decades donated to regional politicians and judges, manage to buy his freedom with just a slap on the wrist, I wondered.

All the local papers and television stations covered my father's arrest. Unbelievably, many people who reached out to me initially expressed sympathy for my father, saying he was just an old man who didn't know what he had done. I told everyone I could that I was the person who'd had him arrested for unspeakable things he had done to me as a child. They ultimately sympathized with my plight but did not give my father the grief he deserved. In fact, patrons of his bar continued drinking with him on a regular basis.

Nor did the media approach me for a statement, although I was interviewed for an online blog. Also, an investigative team from a local TV station interviewed Karyn and me but, much to our dismay, never aired the segment because the Avon Police Department would not confirm that the voice on the recording was my father's. I found it inconceivable that the police would not validate the evidence and the media would not find our remarks credible. Eventually, the scant news coverage there was of my father's arrest died down and he continued on as if nothing had happened, still going to bars and digging in dumpsters without scruples or care for others. Even so, I was relieved to have exposed my father as a lifelong serial molester and to have gone public with my own abuse. Without skipping a beat, I vowed to help criminalize child sexual abuse offenses at the state level and offer a platform and relevant resources for survivors.

Chapter 17

As anticipated, the criminal trial turned out to be not only a long, drawn-out ordeal but, with Karyn and me living next door to my father, three years of sheer hell. At first, anytime I saw him outside I would scamper indoors to avoid interacting with him. Karyn, on the other hand, had no qualms about shouting across the yard, "Hey, pedophile," to which he would shrug and continue with his chores. With more EMDR therapy, I became better able to stand my ground in his presence.

In addition, Karyn and I had to schedule our lives in compliance with the court docket. We ended up canceling numerous RV trips—to places like Thunder Bay, Ontario; the Upper Peninsula, Michigan; and Nashville, Tennessee—because of a pre-trial or magistrate meeting, only to have it rescheduled due to what appeared to be the defendant's delay tactics. For example, one important meeting was postponed because of my father's claim of upcoming "heart surgery," which proved to be an outpatient procedure that could be conducted at any time.

Fortunately, the seven-week RV retirement trip to the Pacific Northwest that Karyn and I had planned to begin in June 2021 came to fruition. We had confirmed the dates in advance with the prosecutor's office and judge and felt assured that procedures for the criminal case were finally coming together. Then the judge had recused himself due to what he called "a family issue," which I'd viewed as an excuse by a recipient of my father's donations. At first, my siblings, Karyn, and I had been livid, but both our lawyer and the prosecutor assured us the recusal would not necessitate another delay. Then my brother had suggested getting my father to settle out of court, but I fervently disagreed, insisting that the audio recordings be played in court for everyone present to hear. A month before our scheduled departure, a COVID-safe Zoom meeting had been arranged so my father could come declare his guilt or innocence. We listened remotely from home as he pleaded no contest, waiving his right to a trial and avoiding an admission of guilt. Though we were disgusted with this outcome, the prosecutor assured us that guilt would be assigned by the judge at the sentencing hearing.

Karyn and I were camping in Washington in July when the hearing took place. That morning we tested the Internet connection at our remote campground several times, discovering that to get the best signal, we would have to set up our laptop on a table outside the laundry room, within range of the hum from the dryer exhaust vent and random laundry patrons streaming by, while off in the distance a beautiful mountain lake. When it came my turn to speak, I read aloud the following statement I had prepared:

> I never imagined that I would be in the situation I now find myself. In September 2018, my world as I knew it came crumbling down. While watching Christine Blasey Ford get cross-examined by irate senators for repressed memories that she'd had years before, small glimpses of abuses that happened to me as a child began to

emerge. By the end of the day, I knew I had to break the news to my wife that I had been molested by my father and mother for years during my childhood.

My memories surfaced in a flood and, to this day, still trickle back to me. My amazing wife has been my rock as I heal from my abuse. She found an amazing psychologist who specialized in treating child sexual abuse victims and told us that my case is the worst she had ever heard.

Sharing this with my siblings, I found out about the abuse of my sisters, the walking around nude, and having sex in front of us as children. My sister Ruth remembers episodes of oral sex—both giving and receiving—plus a picture that was taken, which my father proudly gave her as an adult and which she immediately destroyed.

The trauma that I have experienced is hard to summarize, as I'm sure would be true also for my siblings and my wife. I have been taking an antidepressant; I need Xanax to sleep; my eating disorder has worsened; and I had to take a three-month leave of absence from the job I love because I could not concentrate on my public service work.

My father tried to convince people that it was just me and my mother "messing around." As time has gone on, and the memories have become clearer, I can tell you that my mother and I never had sex alone and that he orchestrated every encounter—from the time I was nine, when he first noticed that I was getting erections and had me share them with my mother, to the time he began having us put our penises into my mother's vagina at the same time. Now, is my mother innocent? Not at all, but she, like me and my siblings, did whatever we were told, any and everything, any and every time. I was, in a sense, the lead actor in my father's personal child abuse production for at least seven years of my childhood, performing acts that occurred hundreds of times.

When I decided to go forward with getting him to confess to these acts, I knew it would be easy. His narcissism is evident on the audio recordings—admitting to acts, my age, and even how small my penis was when things started. Less than a week later, while talking to my sister about the picture he took of her, I had a flashback of him taking a picture of me having sex with my mother. I phoned him about it; he said he still had it. Five minutes later he called with the news that he had found the picture. I then recorded the second event of him giving it to me and stating how old he thought I was at the time.

The evidence in this case is overwhelming. Unfortunately, the statutes of limitation were not in our favor for the physical molestation allegations. With help from our lawyer, Paul St. Marie, and the excellent people at the Lorain County Prosecutor's Office, the decision was made for the pandering child pornography case. I don't want to lessen the seriousness of the child pornography charge, but it pales in comparison to the years of childhood sexual abuse my father perpetrated on me and my siblings. I am grateful that people will finally learn what kind of despicable human being my father is.

Thank you for allowing me to speak.

I was proud to read this statement aloud with my abuser present, listening to every word of it. After I said the phrase "he orchestrated every encounter," he shouted, "That's a lie!" Unfortunately, he was not held in contempt of court for his outburst.

As the judge began announcing the sentence, Karyn and I held hands. My father was charged with a fourth-degree felony, which in Ohio subjects offenders to little more than parole; however, the judge was extremely harsh on him, alluding not only to the pandering of child pornography, on which the charge was based, but indirectly to the molestation as well. At one point he chastised my father for deriving as much pleasure in giving me the photo as he did in taking it. He further stated that a DNA test would be administered—to be used, no doubt, were my father tied to other sex abuse cases—and issued a restraining order requiring my father to stay fifty feet away from Karyn and myself. The judge then asked if that would work for me, to which I replied, "Your Honor, I have spent the past three years trying to avoid him and will continue to."

My father was also sentenced to six months in the county jail. We were stunned, but not nearly as much as my father and his lawyer, who then asked if the six months would be suspended. "No," the judge replied. My father, flabbergasted, stated that he had businesses to run and requested a day to get his affairs in order. The judge replied that he'd had months between pleading and sentencing to do so and that the bailiff would be taking him to jail that day.

The judge's final remark, which I will never forget, was addressed to the bailiff in the hall. "Eddie, are you out there?" he asked. "I need you to come take Root Jr. away." Karyn and I squeezed our clasped hands and tried to look stoic until the proceedings ended. We were not able to see my father taken away, but we did appreciate hearing the judge express sympathy for what I had gone through. Then we danced, kissed, and hugged, elated that the mighty one had fallen. The person who had controlled me for over fifty years had proved fallible, and I felt free for the first time in my life.

A month later, my victim's rights advocate from the prosecutor's office informed us that an appeal was scheduled. We went to the courthouse for it, and this time my father appeared remotely on camera. It gave me pleasure to see him in prison stripes.

The appeal, it turned out, was for health issues. The judge offered to send my father to prison, where there were better medical facilities. The proposal was quickly dismissed and a sidebar requested, at which point my father's lawyers went to consult with him in a separate room. When they returned, the feed showed my father complaining to the corrections officer, "I don't deserve to be in jail." The judge, while seemingly concerned about my father's health but disgusted by his lack of remorse and unwillingness to take responsibility for the crimes committed, denied the appeal. I felt satisfied, less because the appeal was denied than because everyone in the courtroom heard the judge's assessment of my father as a man with no remorse or sense of responsibility.

CHAPTER 18

Living next door to my father's empty house while he was in jail felt refreshing and, in a way, rejuvenating. Karyn and I spent the rest of the summer and fall of 2021 outdoors as much as possible. We planted trees and bushes along the boundary line between the two properties to reaffirm our autonomy from my father. I also used the time to work on repealing Ohio's statute of limitation laws for child sexual abuse and building a platform for male survivors so others in my situation, both locally and nationwide, could get justice.

My research revealed early on that Ohio's statutes of limitations for child sex crimes ranging from ten to twenty years were antiquated, and I wanted to see them repealed altogether. Karyn and I believed that legislatures should be invested less in misdemeanor offenses such as marijuana possession and more in helping victims of horrific crimes. Indeed, we both felt strongly that when a person had irrefutable evidence of a sex crime of any sort, no statute of limitations should prevent legal proceedings, regardless of its severity. It is impossible to guess how much time my father would have received for molestation under such circumstances, given the evidence provided by two audio recordings, a Polaroid photo, as well as testimony from myself and my siblings, but surely, as an eighty-year-old, he would never again have seen freedom.

In most states with antiquated statute of limitation laws against child sex crimes, they were kept in place by two groups: a religious organization with a long history of molestation committed by its clergy and a civic organization with leaders and directors accustomed to molesting its young male members. In Ohio, the effort to keep antiquated statute of limitation laws in place was supported by a third party: a central Ohio college that had been countering sexual abuse charges filed by many student athletes against a staff doctor. With this in mind, I embarked on a phone and email campaign, lobbying Ohio legislators of both persuasions—those staunchly supporting the fight to overturn the antiquated laws and those determined to keep the status quo and protect sexual offenders. Not surprisingly, responses came only from the first group.

Now, after spending more than six years communicating with the Ohio Senate and House of Representatives regarding this issue to no avail, I remain determined though frustrated. No sooner do Democrats introduce House and Senate bills doing away with the statutes of limitations for rape and child sexual abuse than Republicans obstruct the bills so they never make it out of committee. I have had animated conversations with sponsors of these bills, who appear sympathetic to my story and want me to testify on their behalf when the hearings are scheduled. Through social media, I have kept pressure on legislators to hold such hearings. Despite my mounting frustration and the fact that expunging these statutes of limitations will not help my own case, I plan to keep the issue alive until survivors of child sexual abuse in Ohio are able to confront their abusers and our communities are freed of them. Currently, advocacy appears to be growing considerably in favor of ensuring that child predators and those who protect them from liability will not find refuge in Ohio's laws.

In terms of building a platform for male survivors of sexual abuse, the opportunities presented by my father's incarceration were ample. Freed of the anxiety I'd felt with him living next door, I focused on evaluating the available resources, increasing their visibility, and offering additional support for men subjected to sexual violence and battling the underlying feelings of shame still permeating the fabric of their lives, including their emotions, relationships, and behavior. Aware of the #metoo movement's effectiveness for female victims of sexual abuse, I envisioned an equivalent for males who had expectations and concerns of their own, such as the sense of inadequacy as a man (loss of power, control, and self-confidence), stereotypical masculine traits, society's disbelief in such assaults and the resulting pressure to "prove" one's manhood, problems with closeness and intimacy, fear or intolerance of homosexuality, and the pervasive lack of empathy for male survivors.

I set forth on this quest by recalling that while therapy had been instrumental to my healing, I yearned for information, guidance, and support outside of my sessions. Due to the disgusting details of my abuse, there was only so much I could subject Karyn to and only so many close friends I could share them with. I desperately wanted to meet men with similar experiences and learn how they dealt with their trauma and, more importantly, the long shadow it had cast over their sense of self-worth.

Early on, I had reached out to the national organization RAINN (Rape, Abuse & Incest National Network) and was told that its affiliates near me were the Lorain County Nord Center and the Cleveland Rape Crisis Center. But when I called the Lorain County Nord Center I was told that no one there could help a male molested as a child and to reach out to the Cleveland Rape Crisis Center. When I called this organization, I was told it had not heard from a sufficient number of males to warrant holding a support group more than once a year, usually in February. Then, when February arrived without a return phone call, I informed one of its directors that I would like to both start a group for men and be a male contact for others in my situation. Again I received no reply.

Next, I started a meetup group online called the Northeast Ohio Survivors of Sexual Child Abuse. Although seven or eight people joined the group, none attended the initial online meeting. After launching the platform and attempting seven or eight times to hold a virtual meeting, I gave up and suggested that other members run it.

An international recovery program I found to be highly supportive of its members was Survivors of Incest Anonymous (SIA), recommended by my therapist. Because its in-person meetings were held at locations far from my home, I participated most extensively in online teleconferencing, which proved to be highly emotional. It felt good to talk with others—especially males—who, impacted by similar horrific experiences, were dealing with unwanted flashbacks, invasive thoughts, and extreme vulnerability. I discovered that male survivors were drawn to one format or another depending on their needs. Those disinclined to show their faces preferred teleconferencing, while those more open but seeking distance opted for virtual meetings, and those yearning to hug or hold hands with fellow survivors liked face-to-face meetings.

Considerable effort will be required to provide male victims of child sexual abuse with resources targeted to their unique needs. Two principle reasons for this are that many people do not know how to deal effectively with male survivors and others do not know they exist. Actually, they exist in large numbers. RAINN reports that, as of 1998:

- 2.78 million men in the United States had been victims of attempted or completed rape.
- About 3 percent of American men, or 1 in 33, had experienced attempted or completed rape in their lifetime.
- 1 out of every 10 rape victims were male.[1]

Not only are male survivors of sexual abuse present in large numbers, but society tends to blame and shame them. My father's lawyer, for example, made me feel worthless by falsely suggesting that as a young boy I'd been addicted to pornography and a willing participant in the sex acts that overshadowed my childhood. Instead, society must learn to better support those who have suffered at the hands of their abusers. My hope is to bring light to this issue and engender more empathy for male survivors of child sexual abuse.

CHAPTER 19

OUR FINAL LEGAL PROCEEDING was a civil lawsuit against my father for child sexual abuse. Its purpose was less about monetary compensation than to find solace, stand on principle, and punish my father, who had wronged me.

Our chances of success were questionable because in Ohio the statutes of limitations in place for criminal lawsuits involving child sexual abuse extended to civil lawsuits as well. Nevertheless, Karyn and I felt that irrefutable evidence should be pertinent to a case no matter how long ago the events transpired, and fortunately our lawyer agreed and did what he could to help us. For starters, we contacted a lawyer from Cleveland who specialized in cases of a delicate nature like ours, some high profile, and she agreed to meet with us. In contrast to her reputation for being tough, she showed us great compassion while reviewing our evidence and explained that the status of the criminal case was undecided and our civil case stood a much better chance of delivering a guilty verdict. She wanted to know if the abuse could be tied to my father's business, and concluded that it couldn't since I had memories but no proof of being molested at his bar. She then collected our information and the names and phone numbers of my siblings, as well as details about my father's properties and assets to determine the amount of compensation we could ask for. The case she filed for us, alleging abuse, defamation, and other criminal activity was solid and likely to enrage my father.

The typical civil lawsuit games followed, including a long wait and a counter-defamation suit against Karyn and me. Then once the criminal case had ended and sentencing had been handed down, our lawyer proposed moving the civil suit forward but was hamstrung by the defense attorney asking to wait until my father's sentence had been served. And so, in January 2022, when my father was released from jail, he was served papers with a large monetary penalty and a demand to remove his name from the title of the house I shared with Karyn.

Meanwhile, my EMDR therapy continued apace, helping me unfreeze and integrate more childhood memories and deal with related issues that had been disturbing me. I especially wanted to know whether I'd had homosexual relations with my father or sex with any of my siblings, and whether other intense memories were likely to surface. The EMDR sessions took me ever more deeply into my mind to locate and reprocess buried memories. The depths of the darkness I encountered while searching for answers was reminiscent of some of the fiercest fires I had fought. It was as if I were wading through thick black smoke, crouching low through unimaginable heat, feeling my way forward while searching for victims, then emerging before a flickering glow soon to become a raging inferno of "the Red Devil" needing to be squelched with hose, nozzle, and water. Only after working exhaustively with my therapist for several sessions did these encounters lose their emotional charge for me. I became certain that I did not have sex with my father or my siblings. And I learned on a cellular level, that just as I could control my reprocessing of terrible memories through EMDR, so would I be able to defeat the eruption of future inner fires with knowledge and courage.

Our reprieve from having to deal with my father firsthand also ended in January 2022, when he moved back into his house. Initially, Karyn and I were fortunate to not see much of him due to an unusually harsh winter in northeast Ohio. Then in spring, when he stepped out of his house more often, Karyn and I began to wonder how to handle any possible violation of his restraining order. Our lawyer, aware of my dilemma—I had no desire to make him retreat into his house if he was already outside and yet my days of scampering away from him were over—recommended keeping the peace as best we could without bowing to my father. The first violation of the restraining order arose one March morning when I was trimming a tree near the property line. I was tired, dirty, and knee-deep in piles of branches as he pulled into his driveway, got out of his truck, and set to work on a project only ten yards from where I stood. We did not exchange words. I texted Karyn to come video the encounter. We then showed the video to the police, along with a copy of the restraining order. When they arrived to talk to my father, he lied, stating that I had come out while he was already there.

Nevertheless, the incident must have troubled him, because soon after, we received a pre-trial offer from him to settle the civil lawsuit. The document, which pitted me against my siblings for his assets, was unacceptable. While preparing a counteroffer, our lawyer relayed the message that I would have no problem facing my father in a courtroom and testifying to every bit of child sexual abuse that he and my mother had committed against me.

A second violation of the restraining order occurred in August, after we had received an offer we agreed to—which, in my father's mind, apparently entitled him to do whatever he wanted. I was mowing along the property line when he came within ten feet of me and sat down, possibly to do some weeding. I told Karyn that if he was still there when I took my next pass with the lawnmower, we would call the police. As I came by, he stared at me but did not move. For this he could have been taken into custody, but since the settlement documents had not yet been signed, I asked the police to simply give him another warning. When they did, he cursed at them. It was the last encounter I had and, hopefully, will ever have with the man who ruined my childhood.

Once the settlement documents were finally signed, my therapist had me deepen my healing by writing three letters of forgiveness: one to my father, another to the mayor, and the third to myself as a child. At first, I imagined that forgiving my father would be impossible, having idolized him for the vast majority of my life; but knowing that he was seriously deranged eased the way. To him, I wrote:

Dear Father ~
The thought of ever forgiving you was unfath-omable to me before my therapist suggested writing letters of forgiveness as fuel for healing. Seeing you as you currently are—old, hunched over, and not nearly as powerful as you used to be—has awakened sympathy within me but

also taken away some of the joy I felt at winning the civil suit I brought against you. I would much rather have seen you suffer when you were younger and a force to be reckoned with.

I feel sympathy for whatever created you, whether it was a situation with a relative or the pure evil that consumes you. I am not religious and do not believe in a higher power, so I see no chance of a god having created the evil you embody. I also feel sympathy for your shallowness and inability to own your part in the relentless sexual abuse that you, in complicity with my mother, committed against me. But sympathy is not forgiveness.

I offer you forgiveness for my being such a willing subject, for not questioning you, for making it easy for you to be a child molester and, due to my malleability, a very successful one, almost managing to get away with it. I forgive you for the molestation, both to heal my own hatred and to acknowledge your decency at other times, especially when guiding me into the fire service, a career I loved. Finally, I forgive you because your life is now that of a miserable old man and your suffering, though you will never admit it, a force sure to keep you alone and empty until you die.

—FRANK III

Before writing to the mayor, my boss while fire chief, I did not realize how deep-seated my animosity was toward him. But the more I wrote, the more clearly I realized that, while he had not handled my situation properly, he had faced difficult challenges posed by my increasing mental instability, paired with the disturbing nature of my abuse. In short order, I released my feelings of hostility and came away with considerable empathy for him. To him, I wrote:

Dear Mayor ~

I wish forgiving you were as easy as it should be. You have proved to be a shallow little man and at times a bully. You made a career I loved, enriched by a position I held proudly and passionately, a miserable and intolerable job. While you were slowly killing me with stress, I also lost a year's salary and my deferred retirement account benefits. Your apathy toward the pain and suffering I endured after my repressed memories of sexual abuse came back is shameful for an individual whose job is to run a city dependent on loyal and effective employees. I understand that running a city is tough, but you should realize your employees—your most valuable assets— are worth taking care of. The city will be better for it. By contrast, I took great pride in being there for my firefighters when they had troubles or experienced pain. In fact, the last person I had to fire hugged me before he left, because he knew I had always been there for him and was sad that his employment had been terminated.

That said, I forgive you for making me such a lapdog that I bowed down to authority instead of making me the peer I should have been. In acceding to such subservience, I also subjected myself to your insufferable racist and sexist rhetoric.

I forgive you for whatever happened in your younger days that made you the way you are.

I hope you think of the way our working relationship ended and the hollow apology you once gave me. Please learn from it and be a better leader.

—CHIEF ROOT (RETIRED)

Composing the letter of forgiveness to myself as a child was the most daunting part of this assignment from my therapist. Once I started typing, however, the words flowed effortlessly, maybe because I was indeed sorry for all I had put myself through.

Dear Little Frank ~
No one in this world has more of my sympathy and deserves more forgiveness than you. Your life is more disturbing, dismal, sad, and shame-filled than you'll be able to understand until you are much older. Even in my twenties I could not decipher the abuse, and probably would have spiraled out of control if confronted with such memories in my younger days.

I forgive you for wanting the sex and for your willingness to perform. The images of you standing by your parents' bedroom door with an erection, hoping to be invited in, are some of the toughest memories I have to deal with. But I understand all too well how your behavior resulted not only from the physiological desire that gave you those erections and ability to perform but also your desire for the praise heaped upon you for doing so. You were being used by a truly evil person who was, and probably still is, a genius at taking advantage of a weak and young victim.

I forgive you for wanting to be like your father, sexist and racist. I forgive you for how, at your young age, you objectify women while also romanticizing them. You could never possibly understand how demented and shallow your thoughts about women, love, sex, and relationships are since your teachers (parents) are utterly shit.

I forgive you for being a lemming, always willing to do what your father wanted without question. You were totally under his control, through both positive and negative reinforcement. He made you his "big ace" and molded you into what he wanted.

I forgive you for the weight issue, I know how and when it started and hope you someday overcome it. Food was solace for the shame. Shame was the result of orgasms. Orgasms were fulfillment of not only your father's desires but sometimes your own. And the vicious circle continued.

I forgive you for repressing the memories of sexual abuse, which gave you the ability to be fairly normal growing up and ultimately become a very successful adult. Your fortitude in overcoming your initial shame and turning to football to get in shape and gain the strength to finally end the abuse is commendable.

Buck up, little camper. You will survive, you will thrive, and, in spite of being cruelly abused

by two monsters, you will make the most of life
and will get stronger and heal along the way.
—Grown-up Frank

The letters to my father and the mayor were never sent, but writing them, as well as the one to Little Frank, helped me organize my unwanted recognized and even unrecognized feelings about much of the violence that had occurred and see at least some of the searing events through a lens of sympathy. Writing them also helped me release a mountain of resentment and anger. In response, I felt unburdened, uplifted, freed of shame, and much better able to move on.

Once the forgiveness letters were written and the compensatory damages collected, Karyn and I renovated portions of our house and sold it quickly. We then discarded most of our belongings, courtesy of garage sales and gifts to charity, family, and friends; put important possessions in storage; and threw the rest away. Subsequently, in July 2022 we loaded our RV and set forth on the next chapter of our lives, following a vow to heal while exploring the United States and to settle down after finding a new place to call home.

Chapter 20

It has been a year since Karyn and I began exploring the country in our RV. Some people we have met see us as homeless; others, as vagabonds. We see ourselves, however, as travelers on a winding road to recovery, living with greater freedom and a sense that some justice has been served.

My transition since leaving Avon has been remarkable. The nonstop flashbacks, insomnia, anxiety, low self-esteem, and other shame-based symptoms of trauma that once held me captive have given way to an increased sense of being in my own skin. I hike every day with Karyn, have taken up running, lost over seventy-five pounds, and feel physically and emotionally better than ever before. Karyn's love and emotional support have steadily boosted my mental health as well. And I have come to understand that while I may never be completely done with the trauma, it will no longer control or define me, for I know I am much more than that child who was molested for nearly a decade. I'm also able to discern that Karyn, who has helped hold me together throughout this ordeal, was not part of what happened to me in my past. Dealing with this distinction is essential to maintaining honesty in our relationship, bridging the small distances that arise between us, and demolishing the walls set in place when our relationship becomes stressed by my flashbacks. On days when we struggle with either Karyn's traumas or mine, we strive to communicate our individual perspectives and regard each other's issues as equally important, then move on.

In contrast to my new feelings of liberation and healing, I've discovered that not everyone in Avon is happy for us. Some friends and family members view us with animosity, convinced that, having convicted my father and left town in search of sanctuary, we exposed other residents to danger or, alternatively, should never have taken my father on in the first place. I would like to think that in my mid-fifties I am finally able to comprehend people, but in fact I have become less understanding over time and regard anyone harboring sympathy for my father as both unfathomable and reprehensible.

I have also become less insecure and upset when sudden flashbacks of shame-inducing events occur. Fortunately, they are now few and far between, intimating that the longer I am away from places triggering such memories, the likelier I am to eventually be done with them. And flashbacks that months ago might have been devastating are now easily processed in a timely manner. In one, I was eight or nine years old, sitting next to my father at the kitchen table and looking through one of the many interracial sex magazines strewn about the house that day. A photograph that caught my attention portrayed a Caucasian man lying on his back with an African American woman performing oral sex on him. He had his hand on his forehead and, to my naïve mind, looked to be in great pain, so I asked my father why. He glanced at the image and replied nonchalantly, "Oh, he's cumming"—a comment that retrospectively filled me with self-disgust for engaging in such vile conversation until I remembered that the comment had not felt directed toward me. Indeed, EMDR helped me realize that my father's reply was likely self-stimulating banter delivered with no intent to dispel my confusion. Indeed, the meaning of cumming would remain unknown to me for another year or two, when I experienced the stigmatizing experience of my first orgasm in the hotel room with my parents.

Even when unsought, EMDR helps me process bad memories as they surface these days, enhancing my perspective and balance in day-to-day life. A fascinating example of moving spontaneously into an EMDR state occurred one day while Karyn and I were on a fairly moderate trail in the foothills of a Tucson, Arizona, mountain range. While chugging along, captivated bythe rugged landscape, I was suddenly immersed in a haunting flashback set off, no doubt, by the side-to-side movement of my eyes as I scoured our immediate surroundings to ensure safe passage—the same eye motion used in EMDR treatment to recover and process traumatic memories. Frozen in time for a period Karyn gauged as twenty minutes, I grappled with vague memories of a very large naked woman.

For days I wrestled with the woman's identity. Then, one night while in the twilight state between wakefulness and sleep, I became greatly disturbed by a flashback that had me shaking as more details surfaced. I could see my mother coming upstairs to wake me very late at night, wearing a wig and a very short robe, and smelling of alcohol and cigarettes, then ushering me downstairs to have sex. As we entered my parents' bedroom, she took off her robe and led me inside. On the bed with my father was a very large woman with her legs spread open, revealing generous tufts of pubic hair. She was kissing my father and stroking his flaccid penis while he thrust his fingers into her vagina. It was evident that he was unable to get an erection—which I assume was either because he was not attracted to her or had been drinking too much, or because he needed the catalyst of my semen in her vagina. I remember being nervous and feeling that this scenario was all wrong; but my father looked at me and, possibly relieved that I had an erection, urged me to remove my pajamas, climb onto the woman's belly, and have sex with her. I glanced at my parents for assurance that I wasn't doing something wrong by inserting my penis into her vagina, since previously my mother had taken charge of insertions. Seeing them nod in approval, I nervously guided my penis toward the woman's vagina and, finding it, began to perform. As my parents watched, my father's penis became erect and my mother began stroking it. I finished as quickly as I could, put my pajamas back on, and left, aware that the woman's interest was solely in my father, not me. Having previously assumed that the only person my parents had brought into their deviant sexual episodes with me was an attractive woman in her mid-thirties when I was about fifteen years old, as explained in chapter 9, I now realized that my encounter with the large woman dated back to age eleven or twelve, when my bedroom was upstairs. Despite my young age, I doubt I will ever forget seeing her pathetic submission to these perversions, another victim in my parents' sick sex life.

Equally distressing were the lingering beliefs, images, and sensations this memory aroused within me. I was particularly upset to realize that as a youth I was required to have sex with a stranger who could have had a transmissible disease. To this day I have no idea who the woman was and can only assume my parents had picked her up in one of their swinger groups. I knew she was not a barmaid or patron of the bar; if she were, I would have recognized her, since from an early age I had been urged to show my penis to several women at the bar who had been routinely harassed, assaulted, or otherwise coerced into having sex with one or both of my parents. Just as disturbing was the reminder of my father inviting women to have sex with me and them refusing, causing me disappointment and anger. The shame I still feel for my youthful desire to be sexually molested by them is something I have had to repeatedly deal with. It has been difficult to process the anger I experienced as these women turned me down when in fact, as I now realize, they were exercising good judgment.

At the time, I assumed these women shunned the idea of having sex with me because I was fat. Paradoxically, I suspect my weight gain became more pronounced in response to being turned down. Whether it did nor not, my excessive weight did not deter my parents from finding promiscuous women to have sex with me—an endeavor I still cannot fathom. I doubt I will ever understand how parents can molest their children or invite others to. Revisiting how ruthlessly my parents acted on their desires made me see that regardless of any inadequacy on my part—my weight, performance anxiety, or failure to comply with their wishes—there were no limits to what they might have tried.

Corroborating evidence for this new insight emerged soon after, when Remy, our Maltese poodle travel companion, became sick in the RV, unleashing a series of disturbing childhood memories of my father's mistreatment of animals. At our family farm, he took pleasure in slaughtering animals for food, particularly chickens. During one flashback, I could see the joy on his face as he slit their throats while joking about chickens running around with their heads cut off. In another flashback, I saw my father come in the house and, upset that one of our kittens had had an accident on the floor, promptly take the kitty outside and shove a weeding tool into its throat, killing it instantly. I also recalled my father, upon finding poop from our pet dogs outside the house, singing:

> Dog shit, dog shit
> All over the fucking place.
> If Ruthie doesn't clean it up
> I'll shove it right in her face.

I then flashed on a time one of our dogs had accidently pooped in the house, whereupon my father had grabbed a gun, told me and my brother to take the dog behind the barn, then put the gun to the back of its head and pulled the trigger. While watching the life fade from its eyes, I thought that surely, if a family pet could be disposed of so easily, we children could be as well. Only while processing my father's brutality toward animals did I recognize those actions as attempts to cement his control over us and, in particular, his power over me as a sex toy to fulfill his desires.

The source of my most recent flashback—triggered by hearing the word *motherfucker* in a movie—was a crude, humorless joke my father habitually told me during sexually explicit conversations designed to get me aroused for performing his wishes. The joke went like this: "A boy asks his mother, 'Mom, what's a motherfucker?' and the mother says, 'Don't worry about that, son. Just keep on pumping.'" His intimation that I was a motherfucker hardly upset me since I knew that technically I was a motherfucker, largely because I relished his seeming admiration of my sexual activity. What bothered me deeply were what I currently recognize as his manipulation tactics, his sinister use of the word *pumping* to arouse me and his insistence on telling the joke in the company of strangers then watching my face turn red with embarrassment and humiliation. What bothers me now is that the patrons in attendance did or sexual abuse.

Had such intensely disturbing flashbacks to the sex acts I endured rudely interrupted my life a few years ago, I would have been debilitated for weeks, constantly vigilant, fearful of rejection, and feeling isolated and alone. But this past year, with EMDR therapy helping me process them in days, I emerged fueled with hope for increased healing and happiness as Karyn and I continue exploring new locations and more loving and nurturing ways of being.

Once an obedient victim of the abuse I suffered as a child, I have become an activist—in personal therapy, family life, and my connection to the world around me. Whereas I used to take comfort in food—especially burgers, pizza, and ice cream—I currently clear my mind of harsh memories by engaging in a healthy lifestyle complete with hiking, kayaking, long walks, and workouts at the gym. Aware that I am stronger for the sordid events I experienced, I have also begun focusing on two goals to help shape a bright future: dismantling the barriers I have built around myself over the years and welcoming vulnerability as a source of strength rather than a perceived weakness. In this state of vulnerability and at last freed of shame, one of life's most toxic emotions, I have realized that the only person who can truly define us is ourselves. Today I can look at myself in the mirror without shame. What I see is confidence—a man for my wife to love, a father for our kids to look up to, and someone ready to live life to the fullest.

Notes

Chapter 1

1. Admiring and respecting an abuser is a coping mechanism known as Stockholm syndrome, first identified in 1973, by which hostages bond with their captors for the sake of survival.

Chapter 18

1. "Victims of Sexual Violence: Statistics," *RAINN News*, date, https://www.rainn.org/statistics/victims-sexual-violence#:~:text=Millions%20of%20men%20in%20the,of%20attempted%20or%20completed%20rape.&text=About%203%25%20of%20American%20men,completed%20rape%20in%20their%20lifetime.

Resources

Books

Abused Boys: The Neglected Victims of Sexual Abuse by Mic Hunter

Come Here: A Man Overcomes the Tragic Aftermath of Childhood Sexual Abuse by Richard Berendzen

Complex PTSD: From Surviving to Thriving: A Guide and Map for Recovering from Childhood Trauma by Pete Walker

Getting Past Your Past: Take Control of Your Life with Self-Help Techniques from EMDR Therapy by Francine Shapiro, PhD

Healing the Fragmented Selves of Trauma Survivors: Overcoming Internal Self-Alienation by Janina Fisher

The Invisible Wound: A New Approach to Healing Childhood Sexual Trauma by Wayne Kritsberg

Legacy of the Heart: The Spiritual Advantages of a Painful Childhood by Wayne Muller

Reach for the Rainbow: Advanced Healing for Survivors of Sexual Abuse by Lynne D. Finney, JD, MSW

Rebuilding Your House of Self-Respect: Men Recovering in Group from Childhood Sexual Abuse by Tom Wilken

Victims No Longer: The Classic Guide for Men Recovering from Incest and Other Sexual Child Abuse (2nd ed.) by Mike Lew

Waking the Tiger: Healing Trauma by Peter A Levine

Videos

Fire-Brown Gadsden, "Healing Adult Survivors of Child Abuse," TEDxGreenville, May 21, 2016, https://www.youtube.com/watch?v=5viOYkM4CRE.

Tara Walker Lyons, "Surviving Trauma: Without Forgiveness, Can We Still Heal?" TEDxHieronymus Park, April 13, 2020, https://www.youtube.com/watch?v=Gj46FEzDfDQ.

Support Organizations

1in6
https://1in6.org

1in6, focused on the sexual abuse and assault of boys and men, offers 24/7 crisis support from trained counselors, online and phone hotlines, confidential group chats, public policy information, and education.

Adult Survivors of Child Abuse (ASCA)
ascasupport.org

The program for this international self-help support group is specifically designed for adult survivors of physical, sexual, or emotional abuse or neglect. It provides a solid foundation built on research, testing, and participant feedback.

Eye Movement Desensitization and Reprocessing International Association (EMDRIA)
www.emdria.org

This is a professional association for EMDR practitioners and researchers seeking the highest standards for clinical use of EMDR therapy. It is also for individuals interested in information on EMDR or finding a therapist for EMDR treatment.

Help for Adult Victims Of Child Abuse (HAVOCA)
https://www.havoca.org

HAVOCA, run by adult survivors of child abuse, provides support, friendship, and advice for adults whose lives have been affected by childhood abuse.

MaleSurvivor
https://malesurvivor.org

This organization offers a forum for men seeking to come together to heal from sexual trauma. Its offerings include free online resources, moderated discussions, a guide to therapists, a video library, webinars, and both live and online events.

Rape, Abuse & Incest National Network (RAINN)
www.rainn.org

RAINN is the nation's largest anti–sexual violence organization. This nonprofit group operates a 24/7 national sexual abuse hotline and offers programs to prevent sexual violence, help survivors, train consultants, improve public policy, and assist in bringing perpetrators to justice.

Stop It Now
stopitnow.org

This advocacy organization is dedicated to helping families and communities prevent child sexual abuse and exploitation. Its innovative programming is based on a public health model encompassing prevention tools, such as educational materials, podcasts, training services, guidance, and a help line.

Survivors of Incest Anonymous (SIA)
https://siawo.org

An organization devoted to helping survivors become thrivers, SIA publishes relevant literature and holds in-person, virtual, and teleconference meetings to discern delicate issues that plague survivors' daily lives and hinder healing. Meetings are conducted by highly professional, considerate, and compassionate volunteers.

About the Author

Frank Root III was born and raised in Avon, Ohio. Upon graduating from Avon High School in 1984, he joined the local fire department as a volunteer, realizing his childhood dream of becoming a firefighter, like his father. Later accepting a full-time position with the fire department in a nearby town and advancing to the rank of lieutenant, he transferred back to the Avon Fire Department, where he was eventually promoted to chief. On his fifty-fifth birthday, he retired amidst a cascade of incapacitating flashbacks depicting long-buried memories of molestation by his parents. He has dedicated the subsequent years to recovery and cultivating a full life.

Frank and his wife Karyn, a former school nurse, have a blended family with five adult children. Frank and Karyn are currently exploring the United States by RV, in search of a new place to call home. While doing so, they are building an advocacy base for male incest survivors and working with Ohio state policymakers to repeal the statute of limitations for rape, molestation, and sexual assault.